D1513923

To Megan my little friend 29/10/96.
Always cook for fun.
love
Margaret Browne

Through

My Kitchen Window

A Diary of Seasonal Cooking in Ballymakeigh House with
Margaret Browne

Published
by
Ballymakeigh Press

Published in Ireland by
Ballymakeigh Press,
Ballymakeigh House,
Killeagh, Co. Cork
Ireland
Telephone 353 - 24 - 95184
Facsimile 353 - 24 - 95370

© Margaret Browne 1996
ISBN 0 9528838 0 5

Photographs by Daniel O'Connell
and Norma Cuddihy
Typesetting by Rita Scannell
Printed by Colourbooks

For my mother, Catherine (Kitty) Curtin
- the best cook I know!

My thanks to.....

My family, Michael, Michael Junior, Kate, and Theresa,
my friends and guests, for their encouragement, support and taste buds;
Aidan Maguire for planting the first seed;
Daniel O'Connell for his tireless work on the photographs;
Rita Scannell for keeping me sane and mad at the same time;
Patricia O'Dwyer for her faultless typing;
Ann Barry and Anne Deane, my two calm and calming right-hand women;
Tracey Kennedy for the right word in the right place;
Van De Vater for his hunting gear;
Phyll O'Kelly for her invaluable help and advise;
Mary O'Connor for dressing our wine bottles;
Mary Lincoln, Stephen Pearce and Louis Mulcahy for their pottery;
James Brennan & Co., Egans China and Glass Ltd., and The Ballymaloe
Kitchen Shop for tableware and accessories.

Contents

Dinner Menus Page 65

Saint Patrick's Day Dinner Page 66

Easter Menu Page 73

A Romantic Dinner for Two Page 80

Summer Dinner Page 86

Midnight Snacks

Important

All recipes have been tested using Imperial Measurements

Foreword

"You are always working," was the greeting from my friend as she sauntered into my kitchen the other morning. "No I'm not, I'm only making biscuits, and that's not work," was my natural reply. But, my friends, I must confess that those were not always my sentiments. There was a time when I loathed cooking, and for many years I tried every trick in the book to avoid learning to cook real food!

I grew up in rural Ireland during the heady days of the '50s and '60s. Life was exciting and challenging. In a few short years the whole fabric of our society changed rapidly, with the introduction of rural electrification and television, massive E.U. grants, not to mention man landing on the moon, Women's Liberation, The Beatles, Discos, working mothers, sliced pan, fast food outlets, and disposable towels. Stiff upper lips softened and club life was replaced by pub life. The rich aroma of a pheasant casserole bubbling placidly on the kitchen range, or a white soda cake rising steadily in the bastible hanging over the fire, was replaced by a fast takeaway from the local chip shop.

Of course, I must also add that as the youngest member of a family of two, and an only daughter, I was somewhat pampered and was accustomed to wonderful meals being served up without a thought as to their origin.
Life at the stove and the sink, producing mouth-watering treats to tempt our tender palates, was the responsibility of grannies, mothers, aunts, mothers-in-law and top ranking chefs, but not for the ambitious career-orientated moi. When I arrived at Ballymakeigh as a young farmer's wife and a recently qualified nurse and midwife, my culinary skills were confined to being able to fry two rashers of bacon and an egg.

I did not know an artichoke from a runner bean, and cared even less! For variety in our diet I reached for a pack of instant food, added plenty boiling water, and became quite adept at whisking. Anyway, it made a change from the hospital cuisine, with its mysterious grey meat covered with even more mysterious brown sauce and the anaesthetizing smell of boiling cabbage. But we were happy............ or were we ?

Alas, a rude awakening awaited me. Michael, my husband, a member of a family of 12, was accustomed to large, well-cooked, hearty meals served at regular times around the large family table. One evening he gently pushed aside his customary 'high tea' of the two fried rashers and a fried egg which I

had presented to him for about the 100th time. He flashed me one of his unsavoury looks, and not a word was spoken. The apple of my eye was in crisis. I knew the menu had to change, and quickly!
To compound the problem, my mother-in-law, in a spurt of generosity, presented me with a deep freeze. That monstrosity stood by the back wall of my gleaming farmhouse kitchen, locked, snow white and empty. I had no use for it. Pangs of guilt engulfed me every time I passed it.

The solution to that problem presented itself in the form of a persuasive salesman selling beautifully presented frozen meals. Bliss! I bought enough to last us for months! They all tasted the same. The chicken resembled salmon, the sautéed mushrooms resembled tough bits of cardboard, and so on.

Eventually, with our waistlines expanding and our levels of indigestion and heartburn soaring as fast as the food bills, I reluctantly bought a cookbook, attended cookery courses and yes! I was hooked. The rest is history.

My first cooked meal could be described as miraculous. In fact, thousands of meals on, I still marvel at being able to take such inedible products as dry flour, soft butter, raw meat, fish in shells and with them create dishes full of flavour.

My kitchen, which used to be as clinical looking and as sterile as an operating theatre, is now filled to capacity with cook books, magazines, hand-written recipes, notes, stickers, fresh herbs, spices and kitchen paraphernalia of all sorts. Climbing up the culinary ladder, I have had lots of fun, thrills and spills, chopping and changing, chewing, cuts, scrapes, burnt offerings, sheer joy, success, accolades and awards. The awards have been many and varied. They include the Calor Housewife of the Year Award, and The National Award for 'Breaking the Mould of Irish Baking'. In the 80s I changed direction and opened my big and rambling 300 year old farmhouse to guests. Since then we have received The Award for National Breakfast of the Year, and The National Best Guesthouse of the Year Award.

Ballymakeigh House has made its way into some of the most prestigous guide books - John McKenna's *100 Best Places to Stay in Ireland* and the world-famous *Egon Ronay Guide*.
But the greatest award of all is when my family requests home-made chutney, fresh pesto sauce or their favourite curry. That is real success!

In this book, I want to share with you the menus, recipes and little secrets which have often saved my bacon, enabled me to hold memorable parties and given me a taste of success. If I can do it, so can you. These recipes are quick to prepare, work well and are light on the pocket. Think positive, work with confidence and you will succeed.

Margaret Browne

Early Morning...

Early morning in Ballymakeigh is hectic, and indeed sometimes the kitchen is more dangerous than a Soho all-night off-licence! Between alarm clocks ringing, weary looking teenagers appearing out of the woodwork, tantrums over lost socks, missing school books, unfinished homework, or worse, mislaid hairbrushes, my early morning fix of strong tea is a lifesaver.

Of course, on the surface all is calm and serene. Our unsuspecting guests witness a completely different scene. They enjoy the first light filtering through the old-fashioned shutters of the house, watch Bucephalis our mighty peacock strutting around the lawn and the cows ambling in from the rich and green pastures to be milked..........

Swift Breadwinners

One of the luxuries of staying in Ballymakeigh is that you can breakfast when you wish. I usually try to get our daily bread baked before breakfast service. I have no patience with the rise and fall of yeast, so you will notice that my recipes are based on self-raising flour and raising agents such as bicarbonate of soda and baking powder.

Kitty's Brown Soda Bread
Courgette and Walnut Bread
Mike's Sunshine Bread
Light Strawberry Muffins
Orange and Caraway Seed Scones
Leek and Onion Savoury Scones
Sassaroli's Favourite Bread

KITTY'S BROWN SODA BREAD

Who is Kitty? Kitty is my mother, who never uses a bread recipe yet makes the best bread I have ever tasted.

10 ozs (300g) plain white flour
6 ozs (180g) coarse mix brown flour
1 tablespoon bran
1 level teaspoon bicarbonate of soda
1 scant teaspoon cream of tartar
Pinch salt
3/4 pint (375mls) buttermilk or sour milk

7" (18cm) round cake tin.

Preheat oven to 425°F/220°C/Gas mark 7.
Preheat a baking sheet.

Mix the flours, bran, bicarbonate of soda, cream of tartar and salt together in a large bowl. Incorporate as much air as possible. Make a well in the centre and pour in the milk.

Draw in the mixture from the sides with your wooden spoon, and mix gently in a full circular movement until a soft, moist dough is formed.

Knead the dough gently. Put into a round 7" (18cm) cake tin. Cut a cross shape into the top of the bread. Place the tin on the preheated baking sheet in middle of hot oven for 20 minutes. Reduce heat to 350°F/180°C/Gas mark 4 for a further 20 minutes or until bread is cooked.

Test by turning out and tapping the bottom of the bread with your fingers. If it sounds hollow then it is cooked.
Cool on a wire rack.
Serves 6.

Courgette and Walnut Bread

This is the bread that won the National Award for 'Breaking the Mould of Irish Baking'

1lb (480g) strong white flour
2 heaped teaspoons baking powder
1 teaspoon ground mace
1 teaspoon cinnamon
3 eggs (free range if possible)
11 ozs (330g) caster sugar
1 teaspoon vanilla essence
14 ozs (420g) courgettes, trimmed, washed and coarsely grated
7 fluid ozs (175 mls) sunflower oil
8 ozs (240g) coarsely crushed walnuts

2 x 1lb (480g) loaf tins

**Preheat the oven to 350°F/180°C/gas mark 4.
Oil the two tins.**

Sift the flour, baking powder, ground mace, salt and cinnamon
into the bowl of the food processor and whizz.
In a large bowl, beat the eggs with the sugar until they 'ribbon'
well, then add in the grated courgettes and vanilla essence to the
eggs and sugar.
Stirring all the while, mix in the sunflower oil and the nuts and
then, using a slotted spoon, gradually incorporate the flour
mixture into the egg mixture. Divide the mixture equally
between the tins. Bake in a preheated oven for 45 minutes
approximately until cooked.
Insert a skewer to test whether cooked or not. If the bread is
cooked fully, it should come out clean.
Leave the bread to cool in the tins before turning out.
Cut in half inch slices, butter and serve.
Serves 6

Mike's Sunshine Bread

Everyone loves Mike's Sunshine Bread. My son brought this recipe to me from Australia, written on the back of a beer mat!

4 ozs (120g) butter
2.1/2 ozs (75g) brown sugar
Grated rind and juice of 1 orange
3 eggs (free range if possible)
4 ozs (120g) self raising flour
4 ozs (120g) coarse wholemeal flour
2 teaspoons baking powder
2 medium size parsnips
Half teaspoon salt

Preheat oven to 350°F/180°C/gas mark 4.
Oil 1 lb (480g) loaf tin or ring tin.
Put a baking sheet in the oven to heat.

Grate the orange rind and then squeeze the orange (reserve juice).
Wash, peel and finely grate the two parsnips. Set aside.
Beat the butter, grated rind of orange and sugar together until very light and fluffy.
Add in the orange juice. Beat well.
Beat in the eggs, one at a time.
Sift the flours and baking powder into the mixture.
Mix in gently using a metal spoon.
Stir in the parsnips.
Put the mixture into the prepared tin.
Place in oven on baking sheet.
Bake for one and a quarter hours.
Leave to cool in the tin.
Cut into thick slices, plain or buttered and serve.
Serves 6.

Light Strawberry Muffins

Ideal for breakfast. The traditional way to eat Muffins is to pull them apart as opposed to cutting them.

12 ozs (360g) plain flour
3 teaspoons baking powder
Half teaspoon salt
3 ozs (90g) caster sugar
Half oz. (15g) bran
3 large eggs, beaten (Preferably free range)
3 ozs (90g) melted butter (slightly cooled)
8 tablespoons milk
Grated zest of half an orange
8ozs (240g) firm strawberries
(blueberries or raspberries can be substituted)

Muffin tins, lightly oiled, or paper muffin cases.
Preheat oven to 400°F/200°C/gas mark 6

Put baking sheet into the oven to heat.
Oil muffin tins or put paper cases in muffin tins.
Sift the flour, baking powder, salt, sugar and bran into a large bowl. Make a well in the centre. Beat the melted butter, milk and eggs together. Pour into the well of dry ingredients. Stir with a fork, then add the orange zest and fruit. Stir once or twice again very briefly, but be careful not to over beat the batter. Using a tablespoon, spoon the batter into the prepared tins or paper cases. Put tins of muffins on hot baking sheet. Bake in the centre of the preheated oven for 20 - 25 minutes until risen and pale golden coloured on top.
Remove from oven and cool slightly. Transfer to a wire rack.
Serve the muffins hot with butter and whipped cream.

Makes 12

BREAD

Orange and Caraway Seed Scones

16 ozs (480g) plain flour
Three quarters teaspoon salt
2.1/2 teaspoons baking powder
Half teaspoon of bicarbonate of soda
2 ozs (60g) sugar
2 ozs (60g) butter
3 ozs (90g) currants
Grated rind of 1 orange
One and a half teaspoons caraway seeds.
Half pint (300mls) approx. buttermilk.

**Preheat oven to 425°F/220°C/ gas mark 7
Pre-heat baking sheet.**

Sift flour, salt, bicarbonate of soda and baking powder together. Add in the sugar. Rub in the butter until mixture resembles fine breadcrumbs. Add in the currants and caraway seeds. Grate the orange rind finely. Add it to the buttermilk. Make a well in centre of the flour mixture. Add in the buttermilk mixture. Mix well. You should have a lovely soft dough.
Form into a ball. Roll out to about 1 inch (2.5cm) thick. Stamp out rounds with a cutter. Put them on the heated baking sheet. Bake for about 12 - 15 minutes until well risen and golden coloured. Cool on a wire tray. Serve with Cinnamon-flavoured cream - see below.
Makes 12.

Cinnamon-Flavoured Cream

**Half small carton of cream,
Half teaspoon cinnamon.
1 teaspoon icing sugar.**
Whip the cream, add cinnamon and icing sugar.

BREAD

Leek and Onion Savoury Scones

These scones are a perfect accompaniment to soup, especially the Peach, Pepper and Tomato Soup on page 39.

8 ozs (240g) onions, finely chopped
6 ozs (180g) butter (preferably unsalted)
1 tablespoon olive oil
8 ozs (240g) leeks, finely chopped
1 lb (480g) white flour
3 teaspoon baking powder
2 ozs (60g) caster sugar
2 tablespoon mild curry powder
1 oz (30g) grated Parmesan cheese
1 large egg, lightly beaten
A little milk.

**Preheat oven to 400°F/200°C/gas mark 6
Preheat a baking sheet.**

Cook the onions in 1 oz (30g) butter and olive oil until well cooked (I do this in the microwave oven). Combine with the leeks. Place the flour, baking powder, sugar and curry powder in a bowl. Rub in the remaining butter and cheese to form a bread-crumb mixture. Add the onion and leek mixture, then add the beaten egg and bring the mixture together. If it is too dry add a little milk to form a nice firm dough. Turn the dough on to a floured surface and roll out to about 1 inch (2.5cm) in thickness. Cut into diamonds (nicer than rounds). Transfer to the baking sheet, bake in the oven for 15 minutes approximately. Halfway through baking I like to turn these scones as they tend to burn underneath.

Serve with a soup of your choice. They are particularly good with any tomato based soup.

Makes 24

BREAD

Sassaroli's Favourite Bread

After trying this recipe, you will never again want to eat the soggy French bread daubed with garlic butter that we call 'garlic bread'- this is the Original of the Species!
This is an ideal bread to serve at a barbeque.

A group of Italians visit us every year.
This is their favourite bread recipe.
Take thick slices of homemade white soda bread or slices of white loaf bread.
Toast them under the grill on both sides.
Brush with olive oil and then rub with half a clove of garlic.
Serve straight away with any of the pasta dishes.

bíonn blas milis

The porridge next door

ar praiseac na gcomarsan

Always tastes better!

Irish Proverb

BREAKFAST

Eye Openers

Easy Breakfast Muesli
Grainy Porridge
Scrambled Eggs with a hint of Lovage
Melon and Pineapple Jam

Once the bread is safely in the oven I can give my full attention to the cooking of my guests' first meal of the day. I love cooking breakfasts. The kitchen always feels so snug and cosy and warm with the delightful aromas of freshly ground coffee beans, kippers, newly baked bread, and golden orange juice. I find the sound of grilling rashers, sizzling sausages, and the hiss of the kettle a very reassuring symphony of sounds!

Then there is the bustle of the breakfast orders coming from the dining room filled with guests whose appetites have been whetted with the faint vapours from the 'holy of holies'.

As soon as the last morsel of toast is eaten, the sounds of cooking are replaced by the hum of the dishwasher, the clinking of cutlery and the "swoosh" of the sweeping brush..............the day has begun.

Breakfast Muesli

I make up enough Muesli to last for a few days.

8 Weetabix ™
4 ozs (120g) soft brown sugar
2 ozs (60g) chopped hazelnuts
2 ozs (60g) chopped walnuts
4 ozs (120g) sultanas
3 ozs (90g) bran
10 ozs (300g) oatmeal wheatgerm

Break up the Weetabix™. Mix well with all the other ingredients. Store in an airtight container.
Serve with slices of fresh fruit and warm milk.

Grainy Porridge

*I love staying overnight with my friend Mary Madden, as she makes
the most delicious porridge. On special occasions, e.g. at Easter or
Christmas, she tells me she always adds an almond to it. Whoever
gets the almond gets an extra gift on Christmas morning or the biggest
chocolate egg on Easter Sunday morning.
At one time, she used to add a coin to the porridge instead of the
almond, but the resulting dental bills proved too high!*

Here in Ballymakeigh, porridge is definitely the most popular
breakfast cereal so I make large quantities of it. I cook it the old-
fashioned way.
The night before, I steep the porridge oatlets in water. Then, in
the morning, I put 1 cup of the steeped porridge oatlets to 3 cups
of milk in a saucepan and allow it to cook slowly over a low
heat, adding more milk and water if necessary.
I serve it with a swirl of fresh cream and a small teaspoon of
Irish Whiskey or a light sprinkling of cinnamon.

Scrambled Eggs with a hint of Lovage

2 tablespoons of milk
A knob of butter
2 large eggs (lightly beaten)
Quarter teaspoon of crushed lovage.
Salt and pepper
1 slice buttered toast

In a small saucepan heat the milk and the butter together. Add the eggs.
Turn down the heat.
Stir constantly with a wooden spoon until the eggs are cooked.
They should have the consistency of whipped cream.
Add the crushed lovage, salt and pepper.
Serve immediately on hot buttered toast.
Serves 1

Cook's tip:
Lovage is quite a strong flavoured herb which tastes similar to celery.
It is a great addition to soups, stews and casseroles.

BREAKFAST

Melon and Pineapple Jam

I can't think of a word that can fully describe the taste of this exquisite jam. It's glistening golden colour brings the sunshine and dreams of hot exotic countries right on to your table. I like to serve a different jam to my guests each morning so this one makes a pleasant alternative to marmalade.

2 lb (approx. 1kg) honeydew melon, after preparation
One and a half lbs (700g) Fresh Pineapple
Juice of 3 lemons
Two and three quarter lbs (1.25 kgs) sugar

Halve the melon, discard the seeds. Peel and chop it into small chunks.
Halve the pineapple. Remove the skin and the central core. Cut the flesh into tiny chunks (think of an enemy while you are doing this!)
Juice the lemons.
Put the melon, pineapple pieces and any juice from them, and the lemon juice into a large heavy bottomed saucepan. Simmer for 20 minutes, or until the pineapple is cooked.
Warm the sugar in the oven. Add the sugar. Cook gently until the sugar dissolves.
Bring to the boil and boil rapidly until setting point is reached. Remove scum from surface of the jam.

To test for setting:
I make a lot of jams so I use a sugar thermometer. I am sure the jam will set when temperature reaches 220°F. You can also test

for setting by dipping a wooden spoon into the jam.
Remove, and twirl the spoon around until the jam on it
has cooled slightly. Then turn the spoon to allow the jam to
drop from it. If the jam is ready it will set on the spoon. If it is
not ready boil for a little longer.

Allow the jam to cool slightly.

Have sterilized jam pots ready (I wash mine in the dishwasher).
Fill the pots with the jam. Place waxed discs on the jam immediately, then cover immediately, or else allow them to go stone cold
before covering.

Makes approx. 6 pounds of jam.

blais é

Taste it,

Aɣus ciocṛaıḋ ḋúıl aɣac ann.

And it will grow on you!

Irish Proverb

Céad Glóir Leat,
A Dia Ghléigil na bhFlaitheas

A hundred glories to you bright God of Heaven

A thug an bia seo dúinn
is ciall chun a caite

who gave us this food, and the sense to eat it!

Irish Prayer

Elevenses

A great calm descends on the house after the excitement of dealing with breakfast, bills, letters, telephone calls and the guests' departures. Baskets of fresh linen are taken upstairs to service the bedrooms. Row upon row of fluffy white towels blow in the gentle breeze on the outside clothes lines.

By 11.30 a.m. everyone is ready for a well -arned 'elevenses'. We all sit around the scrubbed kitchen table enjoying our own refreshing tipple, be it a mug of steaming hot chocolate, a glass of cool elderflower lemonade or a tumbler full of iced apple juice. The air is always filled with lively banter, and snippets of juicy gossip are digested while we munch on something delectable like Mike's Sunshine Bread. The less sociable of us hide behind the pages of the local newspaper. The evening menu is discussed and planned, shopping lists are compiled, and all too soon we are refuelled and back to our chores.

IS MAIT AN T-ANLANN AN T-OCRAS

Hunger is the best sauce

Irish Proverb

The Secrets

I am constantly asked by my guests for a list of my suppliers as the meat, fish, sauces and soup served here in Ballymakeigh taste so good and are so full of flavour.

The secret is that I use only the freshest ingredients to make decent stocks and I marinate all the meat and fish. 'Too much trouble', I can hear you say. Think again, because all you have to do is put the food in the marinade, leave it, and the marinade does all the work. Then you can sit back and enjoy the compliments!

Stocks

Marinades

French Dressing

Stocks

Clear Stock

I never weigh anything for stockmaking. Clear stock is made from uncooked chicken or veal bones. Chop the uncooked chicken carcasses or bones into small pieces. Then put them into a large upright saucepan with some leeks, a stick of celery, a clove of garlic, a few peeled and chopped onions, a selection of herbs. Cover these with cold water. Bring slowly to the boil and cover. Put on the back burner and simmer slowly for 3 or 4 hours. Cool. Skim off fat. Reserve fat for frying vegetables for soup making.

Golden Stock

If you want a golden stock, take the same ingredients as above but roast them in the oven before cooking. The remains of a cooked chicken are ideal for this type of stock. Never, ever throw out cooked carcasses of any birds without first making stock of them. Put them in a large saucepan, add cold water, vegetables and herbs and proceed as for clear stock.

Brown Stock

Brown stock is made from roasted bones. Next time you buy a joint of any description for roasting from your butcher, ask him to chop up some bones for you - the bigger ones are best. Butchers are always glad to get rid of bones.
Then, when you are cooking the joint or bird, put the chopped bones in the bottom of the roasting tin. Place the meat on top. This does two things:
1) It provides a base for the meat to keep it moist while cooking.
2) It browns the bones at the same time for stock making.
Put the roasted bones, plus the bone from the roast joint, into a

SECRETS

large upright saucepan with unpeeled chunks of onion. Add any root vegetables you have (except potatoes and turnips), a couple of tablespoons of tomato ketchup, unpeeled cloves of garlic, peppercorns, a bay leaf and other fresh herbs. Cover with water, and bring to the boil. Cover these and simmer for 3 or 4 hours. Strain. Place in a cool place and skim off the fat. Reserve the fat for frying vegetables etc.

Vegetable Stock

My first summer job, which lasted for 5 summers, was with a Scottish woman who ran a terrific restaurant nearby. That was nearly thirty years ago, when it was fashionable to cook vegetables in huge pots of boiling salted water. She always reserved the cooking water and drank it with her lunch and advised us to do the same. She said it was great for the skin!!

Vegetable stock is a snip to make and indeed adds a certain freshness to your cooking. Just take the selection of vegetables you have on hand, e.g. carrots, parsnips, celery, leeks, etc. Heat a little butter in a saucepan, add the vegetables and fry them without browning. Add some fresh herbs, e.g. parsley, thyme, etc., cover with water, bring to the boil. Add a little pepper but no salt. Simmer for 10 minutes only. Strain the stock. Always reserve the water left over after cooking your vegetables, and there you have it - a wonderful vegetable stock.

Fish Stock

Fish stock is totally different, in that it does not enjoy prolonged cooking. Ask your fishmonger for fish bones. Ask him to chop them up for you. Rinse them, put them into a saucepan with "white vegetables", e.g. peeled onions, leeks and celery, the juice of 1 lemon, white wine and water. Bring to the boil and simmer for no longer than thirty minutes. Strain. If you would like a more concentrated flavour, reduce the stock by boiling the strained liquid.

Marinades

The two simplest marinades, believe it or not, are milk and oil. Soak chicken and pork overnight in milk before cooking, and spot the difference.

Buttermilk is excellent for marinating beef.

All meats can be marinated in oil. The following is an all-purpose marinade to lift pork, chicken, rabbit, veal and lamb out of the doldrums.

All-purpose Marinade

4 tablespoons oil
4 tablespoons lemon juice
1 tablespoon mustard
1 tablespoon grated ginger
1 teaspoon tarragon, chopped
1 teaspoon parsley, chopped

Liquidize all these ingredients together, pour over the meat and leave for a few hours before cooking, turning it once or twice.

Red Wine Marinade

Beef, venison, guinea fowl and pheasant love a marinade of red wine and root vegetables (except onions). The red wine must be boiled first. Then, pour it over the chopped up raw vegetables. Place the meat in this marinade for a few hours, turning it once or twice.

Yoghurt and Mint Marinade

Yoghurt and mint make a delightful marinade for chicken, pork, veal or rabbit.

Half pint (300mls) natural yoghurt
1 tablespoon olive oil
2 tablespoons chopped mint or chives
2 cloves of garlic, finely crushed to a paste
Half teaspoon paprika

SECRETS

Combine all the ingredients together.
Place the meat in the marinade for a few hours, turning it once or twice.

Honey Marinade

Another excellent marinade for lamb, pork chops, quail or chicken.

Quarter pint (150mls) tomato ketchup
2 tablespoons (30 mls) clear honey
2 tablespoons lemon juice
2 tablespoons oil
1 tablespoon Worcestershire sauce
Mix all the ingredients together. Place on a low heat and warm through.
Put the meat in the marinade overnight.

Store the marinades in screw top glass jars in the fridge.

Fish Marinade

A lovely marinade for fish is to combine half a teaspoon of wholegrain mustard with 1 tablespoon of olive oil and a sprinkling of chopped fresh herbs. Brush fish with this mixture at least 1 hour before cooking. Cover the fish with cling film and refrigerate.

French Dressing

1 tablespoon sesame oil
1 tablespoon groundnut oil
Half teaspoon vinegar
Half teaspoon soy sauce
Pinch of sugar and salt.
Combine all the ingredients together in a screw top jar. Shake well before using.

ᵹo méaᵹaí Ᵹia ᵹo stór,

May god increase your store,

aᵹus ᵹealᵬ ᵹo ᵹeo ná raᵬair

And may you never be poor.

Irish Blessing

A warm welcome for the newly arrived guests

Selection of Muffins (Pg 6).

Opposite right: Kitty's Brown Soda Bread (Pg 3)
and Courgette and Walnut Bread (Pg 4).

Asparagus Spears with melted Butter (pg. 37)

*Opposite right: Brunch Menu - from top left clockwise: Profiteroles with Glossy
Chocolate Sauce, Feta 'between the Sheets', Selection of Irish farmhouse Cheeses,
Beetroot and Apple Salad, Smoked Salmon with Horseradish Creamed Sauce, Tangy
Minted Strawberry and Orange Salad, Apple and Blackcurrant Zingers. (pg. 25)*

Pea Soup (pg.86)

Opposite right: Leek, Tomato and Potato Soup (pg. 49)

Marinated Tomato and Hawthorn Salad (Pg 43).

Opposite right: Baked Turbot Steaks with Redcurrant and Mushroom Sauce (pg 40). Boiled new Potatoes with Mint Pesto (pg 42).

Chicken Ballymakeigh with Saffron Pearl Barley (pg. 46)

Chocolate Layer Pudding (pg 79)

Heavenly Chocolate Cake with Glossy Chocolate Icing (pg. 54)

Celebration Brunch for 12

Selection of Breads
Freshly Squeezed Orange Juice
Apple and Blackcurrant Zingers
Slices of Smoked Irish Salmon, Prosciutto or Spiced Beef
with Horseradish Cream Sauce
Feta Cheese 'Between the Sheets'
Beetroot and Apple Salad
Tangy Minted Strawberry and Orange Salad
Profiteroles with a Chocolate Sauce
Cheese Board with some of our Irish Farmhouse Cheeses,
Milleens, Gubbeen, Ardrahan, Knockanore,
Cashel Blue and Knockalara.

BRUNCH

Cooking for the family is fine, but what do you do when confronted with a celebration such as a post wedding gathering, a christening, anniversary or just a big family reunion? Horror and panic, don't fuss, have a brunch! My choice of recipes for a brunch are really easy to do and can all be prepared beforehand. All you have to do is set up a long table with a nice tablecloth and napkins, a stack of plates and cutlery on one side. Serve the food in large, attractive bowls and platters, let everyone help themselves, and make sure that later they all help you with the cleaning up! Remember, a brunch is served early in the day when the sun shines through every window exposing dusty shelves, vintage cobwebs, etc. so a good spring clean is vital before the arrival of your guests. Wage war on the bathroom and put a nice plant or a bunch of flowers here and there. With the furniture polished and all your preparations done beforehand you cannot lose.

The last brunch I did was nervewracking. Twenty people were booked so everything was ready and organised for them. The tables were groaning under the weight of beautifully presented food. We were so organised that my assistant had taken the day off to attend the All-Ireland Hurling Final in Dublin. Four times as many people arrived. At one stage I counted 90 people! These ravenous revellers had cleared the tables of food in no time, and a queue waited for more food. There wasn't room for them to sit or stand so they were spilling out into the garden, into the kitchen, and some of them were sitting on the deep freeze in the utility room. Fortunately the weather was glorious so one reveller sat on the garden steps playing an accordion, as another was playing his trumpet. The craic was mighty, but there was not enough food. I never experienced such panic in my life. A mad dash to the kitchen garden with a stopover at the herb patch furnished us with the ingredients for the green salads. A quick splash of vinegar, a dollop of oil and a clove of garlic, were all quickly blended together to make a lovely dressing for the salads. There was a frantic phone call to the local cheese producer who came quickly with big wheels of farmhouse cheese. The village shopkeeper thought that the request for 100 thick slices of ham was a joke. Michael, who normally just chats with the guests, was chief cook, bottle washer and waiter. Talk about the miracle of the loaves and fishes, this brunch was more like the miracle of the deep freeze and microwave! Eventually everyone got fed and the brunch was still going on at midnight. There will be days like this.............!

Freshly-squeezed orange juice

Along with potatoes and tobacco, we can thank Walter Raleigh for introducing oranges to Ireland.

Allow 2 oranges per person (24).
Squeeze the oranges.
Orange juice separates so stir it immediately before serving.

> *Cook's Tip:*
> *Valencia is the best juicing orange. Don't throw away the skins. Grate the zest and keep in the freezer for various uses, e.g. in bread, pastas and marinades. Dried in the oven, they make great firelighters, because of the oil in their skins, and they produce great bursts of aromatic flames if thrown on dying embers.*

Apple and Blackcurrant Zingers

9 ozs (270g) fresh or frozen blackcurrants
3 pints (1.8L) pure apple juice.
3 fairly ripe bananas

Liquidize all the ingredients together.
Serve in tall slim glasses.
Serves 12

Smoked Irish Salmon, Prosciutto or Spiced Beef

Arrange overlapping slices of Smoked Irish Salmon, Prosciutto or Spiced Beef on a large platter. Garnish with lettuce and lemon wedges. Serve Horseradish Cream Sauce 'on the side'.
Allow about 2 or 3 slices of each per person.

Horseradish Cream Sauce

    3 small cartons of crème fraîche
6 teaspoons horseradish sauce
3 teaspoons mustard
1.1/2 teaspoons sugar
Salt to taste
6 tablespoons lemon juice

Whip crème fraîche well.
Mix all other ingredients together.
Add to whipped crème fraîche.
Serves 12

Feta Cheese Between the Sheets

This recipe uses filo pastry which is widely available in most supermarket freezers today. It is vital when you are working with filo pastry to keep the sheets that you are not using, completely covered with a damp cloth. I cannot really tell you how much butter to melt - just experiment and you will soon learn how much you need. This dish can be eaten cold also.

**2.1/2 lbs (1kg) fresh spinach or
20 ozs (600g) frozen prepared spinach
6 tablespoons olive oil
6 whole spring onions
1 lb (450g) Knockalara sheeps' cheese or Feta cheese
12 ozs (360g) pot of cottage cheese or Ricotta
3 teaspoons finely chopped parsley
Half teaspoon white pepper
6 medium sized eggs, well beaten
8 ozs (240g) unsalted butter
20 sheets of filo pastry**

                    Roasting tin 28x35x5cm (11"x14"x2")

Thaw the frozen spinach, or if using fresh spinach put it into a big sink. Cover with water, and agitate by hand. Leave it for a few minutes. Any dirt and silt will sink to the bottom. Drain and chop into small pieces.

Heat the oil in a heavy bottomed saucepan.

Add the spring onions and fry until well softened. Add the spinach.

Rinse the Feta cheese or Knockalara cheese under cold water. Break it into bite sized pieces and put in a bowl.

Mix in Ricotta, parsley and pepper.

Add the beaten eggs. Mix very well.

Add spinach and spring onions.

Preheat oven to 350°F/180°C/gas mark 4.

Next prepare the filo pastry.

Paint the roasting tin generously with melted butter.

Then paint each sheet of filo pastry with melted butter as you are putting it in.

Line the tin with about 10 sheets of buttered filo.

Fill with the cheesy mixture. Cover with about 10 more sheets of buttered filo layered on top of each other.

Push the edges of the pastry together around inside of the tin to hold in the mixture. Brush the top with melted butter.

Lightly score the top of the filo in portion-sized squares with a sharp knife. This is to guide you when you cut and serve it.

Bake for 30-40 minutes until golden brown.

Cut into squares.

Serve warm or hot.

Serves 12

Beetroot and Apple Salad

Ready cooked vacuum-packed beetroot is widely available but nothing compares with freshly cooked beetroot from your own garden.

12 medium sized fresh beetroot
6 medium sized sweet apples
Juice of 2 lemons

Wash the beetroot very carefully. Do not break the skins or long roots or they will lose a lot of colour and flavour during cooking.

There are more ways than one of cooking a beetroot.
1) Wrap it in tinfoil and bake in the oven for about 1 hour until tender. Allow to cool. Peel carefully.
2) Wrap it in cling film and cook on high in microwave for 15 minutes. Again allow to cool and peel.
3) Put it in a saucepan. Pour in sufficient boiling water to cover. Cover saucepan. Boil gently until tender, 1 - 2 hours.
4) Cooking beetroot in a pressure cooker is also very good and here is my rough guide: Set cooker at 15 lbs pressure: small beets, 15 mins, medium beets, 20 mins, large beets, 35 mins. Leave in cooking water until cold enough to handle.

Juice the lemons.
Peel and grate the apples and mix in lemon juice to prevent discoloration. Cut the beetroot into chunks and add to the apples. Toss in honey cream dressing.

Honey Cream Dressing

3 tablespoons honey
6 tablespoons cream
Pinch of cinnamon and nutmeg

BRUNCH

Blend all ingredients together.
Just before serving, add the Honey Cream Dressing.
Season and serve.
Serves 12

Cook's tip:
Lemon juice will clean your fingers after skinning beetroot or handling blackberries.

A Tangy Minted Strawberry and Orange Salad

This salad also makes a lovely dessert served with fresh cream or a rich ice-cream.

9 oranges, peeled and segmented
2 punnets fresh ripe strawberries

Tangy mint dressing:
1 oz (90g) fresh chopped mint
1 teaspoon sugar
1.1/4 fl.ozs. (35 mls) wine vinegar
1 tablespoon water

Using a sharp knife, peel and segment the oranges over a bowl to trap any escaping juice.
Halve and quarter the strawberries and place them in a glass serving dish with the oranges. Chill.
Combine the mint, sugar, and wine vinegar together. Liquidize.
Just before serving, pour the dressing over the fruit. Serve immediately.
Serves 12

BRUNCH

Profiteroles with a Glossy Chocolate Sauce

Choux pastry is one of my favourites. It is easy to make, lasts for ages and freezes perfectly unfilled. For large numbers make the pastry in two batches.

The secret of choux pastry is to remember that it is a loner and must be the sole occupant of the oven while it is cooking. The only time I use margarine in cooking is when making choux pastry. It is also better to overcook it rather than undercook it.

6 ozs (180g) margarine
3/4 of a pint (450 mls) of water
7.1/2 ozs (200g) sieved self -raising flour
6 large eggs
Half teaspoon salt

Preheat oven to 425°F/220°C/gas mark 7.
Lightly grease 3 baking sheets. Sieve the flour on to greaseproof paper, cut the margarine into pieces. Place the margarine and water in a heavy based saucepan over a moderate heat. Allow the margarine to melt before the water boils. Bring quickly to a rolling boil, and remove from the heat.
Add all the flour immediately and beat vigorously with a wooden spoon, then return to a low heat for 1 minute. Beat the mixture until a ball forms and will leave the sides of the saucepan.
Take off the heat and transfer the mixture to the food mixer. Using the H beater, beat one egg into the choux mixture and only then beat in the other eggs. Add them slowly to the dough until it becomes smooth and shiny. At this stage, more egg may be

required. When perfect, the choux should be smooth and shiny and fall easily from the spoon.

Spoon or pipe the mixture into mounds on to a baking sheet. The mounds should be about one inch thick.

Leave spaces between each mound and prick each one with a fork and sprinkle with water.

I always put a dish of water in the oven while the choux puffs are cooking.

Bake for 15 minutes, then reduce oven temperature to 325°F/160°C/gas mark 3 for a further 20 minutes.

Open oven door very gently and if the puffs are well risen and golden brown, take one out. If it collapses, give the remainder a further 5 to 10 minutes cooking time.

Remove them from the oven, slit each puff and cool on a wire rack. Scoop out any uncooked dough and discard.

Choux puffs can be frozen or stored in an airtight container. Refresh in oven before using.

Just before serving, fill with whipped cream flavoured with vanilla essence and dust with icing sugar or ice with the Glossy Chocolate Sauce below.

Makes 16 profiteroles

Glossy Chocolate Sauce

6 ozs (180g) best quality chocolate
3 ozs (90g) unsalted butter
1 teaspoon golden syrup
3 ozs cream

Break the chocolate and place with the unsalted butter and golden syrup in a heatproof bowl. Place over a saucepan of simmering water and stir until all ingredients are melted. Add the cream. Stir well. Pour over the profiteroles.

ʒo ꝺꞇuʒᴀ ꝺıᴀ ꝺeocꜧ ꝺuıꞇ

May God give you drink

ᴀꜱ ᴀn ꞇoꝺᴀʀ nᴀcꜧ ꝺꞇʀánn.

from the well that never runs dry

Old Irish Blessing

Lunches

With the hustle and bustle of family life on a busy farm, lunch is often a neglected luxury until the weekend comes around. During the week, we might grab a bowl of soup, or make a quick sandwich to fill the gap, but when Sunday arrives we make a special effort.

These following recipes cater for all sorts of lunches in every season, - whether it is a quick mouthful needed in transit or a leisurely three hour affair with family and friends.

Light Lunches or Starters
Asparagus Spears with melted Butter and Red Pepper Rings
Broccoli and Sorrell Soup
Peach, Pepper and Tomato soup

Midsummer Menu
Baked Turbot Steaks with Redcurrant and Mushroom Sauce
Boiled new Potatoes with Mint Pesto
Marinated Tomato and Hawthorn Salad
Apple Roulade with Apricot and Southern Comfort Sauce

Autumn Comfort
Chicken Ballymakeigh with Saffron Pearl Barley
Boozy Bananas

Post-Christmas Lunch
Leek, Tomato and Potato Soup
Pork Parcels
Turnips the Boss's way
Simple Bio-Yoghurt Restorer

is feaRR leat bulóg

Half a loaf is better

ná beit gan aRán.

than no bread.

Irish Proverb

Asparagus Spears with Melted Butter and Red Pepper Rings

LUNCH

There is a special time in May when the local organic vegetable supplier peeks through the kitchen window clutching his baskets of fresh asparagus spears covered with damp newspapers. It heralds the certain arrival of summer.

20 fresh slender asparagus spears
Boiling water
Half a red pepper
4 ozs (120g) butter melted
Salt and pepper
4ozs (120g) toasted sliced almonds
Squeeze of lemon juice

Select slender spears. (They are more tender)
Snap off the toughest end - they will automatically break where the toughness stops.
Bind the bundles with a piece of string.
Take a fairly small saucepan and fill it with salted water. Boil.
Place the bundles of asparagus standing up into the saucepan.
Invert another saucepan over the top for a cover - this gives you the height you need.
Cook for 3 or 4 minutes until the spears are cooked 'al dente' (with a bite). Do not let them over cook or they will be ruined.
Just before the end of cooking time slice thin circles of red pepper. Add to the asparagus for a few seconds.
Drain asparagus. Stir 4 ozs of toasted sliced almonds and a squeeze of lemon juice into the asparagus.
Slip 5 spears through each red pepper ring.
Drizzle with melted butter and serve with white soda bread, or white crusty rolls.
Serves 4

Cooks tip:
This method concentrates the flavour in the water so retain this water for making soups and sauces.

Broccoli and Sorrel Soup

8 ozs (240g) broccoli
1 large potato
1 stalk of celery
Half clove of garlic
1oz (30g) butter/fat from top of stock
3 ozs (90g) lettuce or spinach
1 large onion
Half pint (300mls) white wine/dry sherry
1 teaspoon mustard
Salt and pepper
One and a half pints (900mls) of really good chicken stock
5 ozs (150g) sorrel
You can use 8 ozs lettuce or spinach instead
Juice of one lemon
1 tablespoon sugar
Some chopped chives
Tiny slivers of red pepper to garnish

Wash and shred broccoli leaves and florets .
Chop the broccoli stems quite finely as they are difficult to cook.
Wash peel and chop potato. Chop celery stalk, and crush garlic.
Place the butter in a heavy bottomed saucepan. When it foams,
add the potatoes, onion, celery and crushed garlic. Cover and
sweat over a gentle heat for five minutes until butter or fat is
absorbed.
Now add in broccoli, white wine, mustard, salt and pepper and
cook again for about 5 minutes. Then add in chicken stock. Cook
until all vegetables are soft. Add the sorrel leaves. Cook for a few
more minutes. Liquidize. Taste, season with a little lemon juice,
salt, pepper and sugar. Thin with water or stock if necessary.
Garnish with tiny wafer-thin slivers of red pepper.
 Serves 4

Peach, Peppeʀ anƆ Tomaᴛo Soup

This soup would be ideal for a nippy August afternoon.

LUNCH

2 ozs (60g) unsalted butter
8 ozs (240g) onions
1 red pepper, finely chopped
1 clove of garlic (pounded to a paste)
2 X 14 ozs (397g) tins of tomatoes
3 ozs sherry (optional)
1 tablespoon caster sugar
3 tablespoons chopped fresh mint
(or one and a half tablespoons dried mint)
1 bay leaf
2 very ripe fresh peaches
1 - 2 pints (600mls -1.2L) good quality stock
Salt and pepper
4 teaspoons of pesto sauce (pg 60)

Melt the butter in a heavy bottomed saucepan. Add onion, pepper
and garlic. Cover, cook gently until softened but not coloured.
Add the tomatoes, sherry, sugar, mint and bay leaf.
Stir together, cover with a lid, simmer for about 45 minutes.
Stir occasionally. Take out the bay leaf.
Liquidize the soup and sieve it or just liquidize it and leave the seeds
in.
Either way peel, stone and chop the peaches.
Add the peaches to the soup and liquidize.
It is now time to add the stock so add it carefully, making sure the
soup does not end up too watery. Bring to boil.
Season to taste with salt, pepper and sugar.
Swirl a teaspoon of pesto sauce (pg. 60) on each bowl of soup.
Serves 4

Cook's tip:
Crush garlic by placing it on a chopping board with a little salt. Then pound it
with a heavy knife or a wooden spoon to form a smooth paste.

Mid-Summer Madness

This is a spectacular lunch menu to celebrate one of the most ancient feasts - The Summer Solstice - or Midsummer Day on June 21st when the Sun, that elusive golden ball in the sky, is at its highest point.

Baked Turbot Steaks
with
Redcurrant and Mushroom Sauce
New Potatoes with Mint Pesto
Marinated Tomato and Hawthorn Salad
Cardamom Apple Roulade
with Apricot and Southern Comfort Sauce

Baked Turbot Steaks napped with a Redcurrant and Mushroom Sauce

This dish looks gorgeous, tastes unique and is very easy to cook.
The sauce would be superb with any robust white fish, such as cod, pollock or hake.
Turbot is definitely one of the finest flat fish. It is easily recognized by the small, bony tubercules on its dark surface and the total absence of scales.

4 Turbot steaks,
each weighing between 8 - 10 ozs (240 - 300g)
1 oz (30g) butter
Salt and pepper
Juice of half a lemon or lime

Redcurrant and mushroom sauce:
1.3/4 pts (1 ltr) fish stock
1 small leek, chopped
1 teaspoon. fresh thyme
1/4 pint (150mls) redcurrant jelly
1/4 pint (150mls) crème fraîche
4 ozs (120g) sliced mushrooms
Bunch of redcurrants

Preheat oven to 400°F/200°C/gas mark 6

Wipe the steaks thoroughly. Paint with a little marinade. (page 23)
Place the turbot steaks on a buttered baking dish. Sprinkle with
lime or lemon juice and season with salt.

Put a pat of butter on each steak (low fat if preferred). Add a
little water to the dish. Cover with greaseproof paper and bake
for about 15 to 20 minutes.

Reduce heat. Make a small incision in the fish to check if it is
properly cooked. If it looks raw continue cooking for a few
minutes more.

Meanwhile, make the sauce by melting the butter, adding the
leek and thyme and cooking over a low heat until the leek is
softly cooked.

Then add the fish stock and redcurrant jelly. Reduce to half its
volume by rapid boiling.

Remove from heat and stir in the crème fraîche.

Fry off sliced mushrooms quickly and add to the sauce.

When the fish is fully cooked, remove from baking sheet and
pour any juices into the sauce.

Add fresh redcurrants (whole) to the sauce. Then pour the sauce
over the cooked fish and sprinkle lightly with chopped chives.
Serve with boiled new potatoes and Mint Pesto (overleaf) .
Serves 4

Boiled New Potatoes with Mint Pesto

As many new potatoes as you need

For Mint Pesto:
Some fresh mint leaves
A few sprigs parsley
3 cloves garlic
Half teaspoon salt
Some fresh black pepper
Quarter pint (150 mls) olive oil
Two and a half ozs (75g) nuts of your choice,
preferably pine kernels or pistachio nuts
4 ozs (120g) freshly grated parmesan cheese
1 oz (30g) soft unsalted butter

Scrub and rinse the new potatoes - the skins should come off easily.
Place in a saucepan and barely cover with lightly salted water.
(1 teaspoon salt to each pint of water.) Boil gently for about 20 to 30 minutes until almost cooked. Test with a skewer then strain off the water and cover the potatoes with a clean tea towel and the lid of the saucepan.

Make the mint pesto by filling the bowl of the food processor with fresh mint leaves and parsley. Combine all the pesto ingredients except the butter and the cheese in the processor and whizz briefly.
Add the cheese and butter by beating in by hand.
Now your pesto is ready. It's as easy as that!
Toss the potatoes in the pesto, serve immediately.
Serves 4

> **Cook's tip:**
> *I usually make a big jar of pesto at one time. I place a layer of non-PVC cling film over the top to prevent fermentation. Store it in the fridge. You can also freeze pesto quite successfully as long as you wait until after thawing to add the Parmesan cheese and butter.*

Marinated Tomato and Hawthorn Salad

These may look like unusual partners but they make a perfect marriage.

4 large, ripe, plump tomatoes
1 handful of young, fresh hawthorn leaves and buds
A little olive oil

Slice the tomatoes. Ripe Irish tomatoes usually taste lovely on their own but feeble imported ones will benefit greatly from a light sprinkling of sugar and salt. Put them in a salad bowl. Wash the hawthorn leaves and buds well and dry. Add to the tomato salad. Drizzle with a little good olive oil and serve immediately.
Serves 4

> **Cook's tip:**
> *Slicing tomatoes takes the edge off knives, so always use an old kitchen knife for the job. Do not wash sharp knives in the dishwasher as this also dulls the edge.*

Cardamom and Apple Roulade

This is a very easy dessert to make, and it is as light as a feather. The cardamom seeds add an unusually exotic taste.

3 ozs (90g) plain flour
3 ozs (90g) caster sugar
3 eggs, preferably free range
20 green cardamom pods (use the seeds only)

For the filling:
8 ozs (240g) cooking apples, peeled and chopped
1 oz (30g) sugar
Quarter pint (150mls) of whipping cream

8" x 12" swiss roll tin
Heat oven to 400°F/200°C/gas mark 6

Line the swiss roll tin with baking parchment.
Remove the cardamom seeds from their pods. Crush the seeds.
If you do not have a pestle and mortar put the seeds with a little of the flour on a plate. Crush them with the back of a soup spoon. Add them to the flour.

Place the eggs and sugar in a bowl over a saucepan of simmering water. Do not let the bowl touch the water. Using an electric hand whisk, whisk the mixture until it is really thick and creamy and holds a figure of 8 when the whisk is drawn over it.
Remove the bowl. Continue to whisk for a little longer.
Very gently fold in the flour using a metal spoon.
Put the mixture into the lined swiss-roll tin. Level it off.
Bake for about 14 minutes.

Turn the sponge out on to a sugar-coated sheet of baking parchment.
Very gingerly remove the lining paper.
Roll up the swiss roll loosely.
Meanwhile, make the filling.
Stew the apples with the sugar and a little water.
Mash to a purée.
Whip the cream. Fold the apple purée into the cream.
Now unroll swiss roll again.
Spread the cream and apple mixture evenly over the swiss roll.
Re-roll carefully.
Serve plain or with an Apricot and Southern Comfort Sauce (below).
Serves 4

Apricot and Southern Comfort Sauce

1 small tin of apricots
2 tablespoons Southern Comfort

Liquidize together. Dilute with a little water if you think the sauce is too thick.

Cook's tip:
Free range eggs must be at least 3 days old for baking.

LUNCH

Chicken Ballymakeigh with Saffron Pot Barley and Chutney

1 oven ready roasting chicken (free range if possible)
1 orange
1 red and 1 green pepper
1 lb (500g) onions
3 cloves of garlic
Salt
Black pepper
6 tablespoons olive oil
1 sprig of fresh thyme
1 sprig fresh marjoram
14 oz (397g) can tomatoes
Pre-heat the oven to 350°F/180°C/gas mark 4

Wipe and quarter the orange. Cut the peppers into quarters.
Peel and slice onions very thinly. Crush garlic to a smooth paste
with salt. Wipe the inside of the chicken. Sprinkle salt and
pepper both inside and outside chicken. Heat the oil in a large
seven pint (4L) flameproof casserole. Add chicken and brown all
over. Remove chicken. Add onions, garlic and herbs and fry for
about three minutes. Return chicken to casserole, breast side
down. Add orange, peppers and can of tomatoes. Bring slowly
to the boil. Season. Cook for one and a half hours at
350°F/180°C/gas mark 4 or until chicken is cooked.
Serving suggestion:
Carve chicken into joints. Arrange portions of chicken, peppers,
orange and tomatoes on hot plates with helpings of saffron pot
barley and chutney of your choice.
Skim the fat off the juice. Pour the juice over the pot barley.
Mix well.
Serves 4

LUNCH

Saffron Pearl Barley

Pearl or pot barley makes a welcome change from rice, pasta and potatoes. Try substituting it in other dishes too.

8 ozs (240g) pearl or pot barley
3 or 4 threads of saffron
8 ozs (240g) sliced onions, thinly chopped
2 cloves crushed garlic
Olive oil
Salt and pepper to taste
1 oz (30g) raisins
1 oz (30g) flaked almonds
1 X 14 oz. (397g) tin tomatoes
Half pint (300 mls) stock

In a heavy saucepan heat a little olive oil.
Fry onions and garlic for five minutes. Add pearl barley, fry for a further three minutes stirring continuously. Powder saffron threads. Add to onions with raisins, almonds and tomatoes.
Boil stock. Add it to the pearl barley. Bring to the boil. Cover.
Simmer for one and a half hours stirring occasionally. You may need to add extra stock. Do not allow the barley to dry out. **Serves 4**

Boozy Bananas

4 bananas, just ripe
6 teaspoons butter
6 teaspoons sugar
2 dessertspoons Grand Marnier
2 dessertspoons light rum
4 scoops of a favourite ice-cream or Greek yoghurt.

Melt the butter and sugar on a low heat. Add the sliced bananas.
Cook very gently. Add the Grand Marnier and rum. Increase heat.
If you have the courage, set the sauce alight!
Serve immediately with a scoop of ice-cream or a serving of Greek yoghurt.
If you are cooking these for children, omit the booze! **Serves 4**

Post Christmas Lunch

After Christmas we all suffer from a little palate fatigue. The days get longer and we can feel Spring approaching but we are still getting the odd nip in the ear from Jack Frost. We need warm, restoring dishes to keep our spirits up.

Leek, Potato and Tomato Soup
Pork Parcels
Turnips the Boss's Way
Bio-Yoghurt Restorer

Leek, Tomato and Potato Soup

1 lb (480g) leeks
2 ozs (60g) butter or fat from the top of the stock
1 X 14 oz (397g) tin of tomatoes
1.1/2lbs (700g) potatoes
1 tablespoon sugar
2 pints (1.2 L) stock
Salt & pepper
1 teaspoon ground nutmeg
1 tablespoon horseradish sauce
2 teaspoons chopped parsley

Prepare the leeks by removing the green leafy parts.
Turn each leek upside down. Holding it in your left hand insert a
sharp knife 1 inch from base of the leek, slit each one in half
lengthways, then in quarters. The leeks will split open yet still be
held together at the base. Put them under the cold water tap and
it will then be easy to clean and wash away any dirt and grit
lurking in them.
Slice the leeks diagonally. Scrub, peel and dice the potatoes.
Melt the butter or fat in a heavy saucepan until foaming. Add
the leeks first.
Cover with a tight fitting lid and cook gently.
Add the tinned tomatoes and cook for a few more minutes. Then
add the peeled and diced potatoes.

Season, add the sugar and stir well. Add the stock and cook
until the vegetables are soft.
Liquidize. Add the horseradish sauce and the nutmeg.
Test for seasoning.
Dilute the soup with water if you feel its consistency is too thick.
Serve in warmed soup bowls with parsley sprinkled on top.
Serves 4

Pork Parcels

4 lean pork chops
1 red onion (sliced)
8 ozs (240g) mushrooms (thickly sliced)
1 oz (30g) butter
5 tablespoons pure apple juice
4 tablespoons cider vinegar
2 teaspoons lemon juice.
1/4 pint (150mls) crème fraîche or natural yoghurt.
Salt and pepper
4 sprigs fresh thyme

As usual, marinate the pork chops overnight
(see pages 22 & 23 for marinades)
Prepare red onions and mushrooms. Slice.

Preheat oven to 350°F/180°C/gas mark 4.
Oil four 12" (30 cms) squares of kitchen foil.

In a heavy frying pan, melt the butter and fry the chops on both
sides until lightly browned - about three minutes each side.
Transfer each chop on to the oiled tinfoil.
Add the onions and mushrooms to the pan and fry until soft.
Stir in the apple juice, cider vinegar and the lemon juice.
Bring to the boil and reduce by boiling to half its volume.
Stir in the crème fraîche or yogurt, salt and pepper.
Spoon the sauce over the pork chops, topping each one with a
sprig of thyme.
Seal the parcels and bake in a preheated oven for about one hour.
Serve in their parcels. **Serves 4**

Turnips 'The Boss's Way' !!

1 small turnip
1 oz (30g)of breadcrumbs
1 knob of butter
Salt & pepper
Pinch of nutmeg
1 egg white
1 capful of brandy

Prepare the turnip by peeling and cubing it. Cook in boiling
salted water until soft, then drain and mash. Put the breadcrumbs, butter, salt, pepper and nutmeg in a casserole dish with
the drained, mashed turnip. Mix well. Beat the egg white and
add to the mixture. Stir in the brandy. Bake in the oven for about
20 minutes and serve.
Serves 4

Simple Bio-Yoghurt Restorer

This is an antidote to the booze and antibiotics of the Winter spell.
Look for the words 'bio' or 'active' on the carton, when buying yoghurt.

4 cartons natural Bio-yoghurt
4 tablespoons homemade raspberry jam
Some chopped walnuts

Pour the yoghurt into four tall glasses.
Top with jam and sprinkle with chopped walnuts.
Allow to rest for about half an hour before serving.
Decorate with sprigs of lemon balm or sweet cicely. **Serves 4**

bíonn blas ar an mbeagán.

A little bite can taste delicious.

Irish Proverb

Lazy Times.....

.....Afternoon Tea

Straight after lunch, a brisk walk will bring me to the stream, the Aodhchán, which flows through our land, and to heavy scented hedgerows. I always return laden with fresh buds, berries, flowers or herbs to enhance the evening dinners.

The afternoon is always very busy with the arrival of guests and the preparation of food for dinners and high teas going on simultaneously. While the vegetables and cooks are sweating in the kitchen, the guests relax in the flower-filled conservatory sipping afternoon tea, snoozing or reading a book. I like to indulge them with lots of little treats. The all-time favourite is Heavenly Chocolate Cake.

Heavenly Chocolate Cake

6.1/2 ozs (195g) plain sifted flour
2 level tablespoons cocoa powder
1 level teaspoon bread soda (Bicarbonate of soda)
1 level teaspoon baking powder
2 free range eggs
5 ozs (150g) caster sugar
2 tablespoons golden syrup
1/4 pint (150mls) sunflower oil
1/4 pint (150mls) milk
Pinch salt

8 inch (20cm) round cake or springform tin.

Preheat oven to 325°F/170°C/gas mark 3.
Preheat baking sheet.

Prepare the tin by brushing with melted butter. Mix a spoon of sugar and flour together and sprinkle evenly around the inside of the tin. Tap it around to cover the base and sides of the tin. Place the flour, cocoa powder, bread soda and baking powder in the bowl of a food processor or blender. Whizz for a few seconds.

Meanwhile, beat the eggs separately and add them with the sugar and golden syrup to the mixture in the bowl.
Process for a few seconds.
With the motor running, pour in the oil and milk and continue processing for a few seconds more. Now the cake is ready.

AFTERNOON TEA

Don't worry if the mixture appears liquidy before cooking.
That is the way it is supposed to be.
Pour the cake mixture into the tin, place tin on hot baking sheet
and bake in the centre of the oven for 50 - 60 minutes approxi-
mately until fully baked.
Leave in tin to settle and then cool on a wire tray.
Serves 8 at least, depending on the level of chocoholism!

Glossy Chocolate Icing

6 ozs (180g) best quality chocolate
3 ozs (90g) unsalted butter
1 teaspoon golden syrup

Break the chocolate and place with the unsalted butter and
golden syrup in a heatproof bowl. Place over a saucepan of
simmering water and stir until all ingredients are melted.
Ladle the lukewarm icing on to the cake, spreading it evenly
over the top and sides.

Cook's tip:
You know that a sponge cake is baked when it begins to recede from the
sides of the tin. Press the centre and it should spring back quite easily.

Muna mbír i otiş an bia

If you are not in a house that has food,

bí ins an tiş len a taob.

be in the house next door!

Irish Proverb

You won't have to worry about the proverb opposite if you're staying in this house! Ballymakeigh House seen here in the spring sunshine

Poached fillets of John Dory with a Citrus Sauce (pg 62)

Trio of Cod, buttered Mangetouts & Warm Orange Segments (pg. 67)

Rich Orange Ice-Cream with Grand Marnier Sauce (pg. 88)

Opposite right: Romantic Dinner for Two. Crab Salad in Red Dresses with a Fresh Herb Sauce, Sizzling Roast Duck with a Rich Wine Sauce. (pg. 80)

Chicory, Orange and Passionfruit Salad (pg. 95)

Opposite right: Nice Bites from the No-Hassle Supper for 10 (pg. 90)
Clockwise from top left: Cornucopias of Smoked Salmon, Olives, Parsnip
Crisps, & French Bread spread with Pesto.

Spaghetti with Basil Pesto Sauce (pg. 60)

HIGH TEA

High Teas on a Low Table

Seasons may change, but certain things remain constant, such as the provision of high teas. If we are not cooking a formal dinner, then the family would always have a high tea instead.

Apricot-Glazed Ham Steaks
Fluffy Parsnips and Parsnip Crisps
Potatoes à la Boulangère
Penne with Five Cheeses
Linguine, Buccatini or Spaghetti with Pesto
Poached John Dory with Citrus Sauce
Sautéed Potatoes with Balsamic Vinegar
Herbed Mayonnaise

Ham Steaks with Apricot Glaze

4 ham steaks
3 ozs (90g) Apricot jam
Half teaspoon cumin powder
2 ozs (60g) French dressing (See Page 23)
1 tablespoon of Sherry

Heat the jam, cumin, French dressing and sherry in a saucepan.
Pour over the ham steaks. Marinate for a couple of hours. Fry or
grill the ham steaks on both sides until cooked.
Serves 4

Fluffy Parsnips and Parsnip Crisps

5 parsnips
Knob of butter
Salt and pepper
2 tablespoons wholegrain mustard
Groundnut oil for frying

Wash and prepare parsnips and reserve one for the crisps.
Cook the parsnips in a little salted water and then drain and
mash with butter, salt and pepper. Beat in the wholegrain
mustard and serve piping hot with the parsnip crisps arranged on
top.

Parsnip Crisps

Peel the parsnips with a potato peeler. Continue peeling to get
long thin strips of parsnip. Put these somewhere warm to dry
out. Just before serving, heat the groundnut oil. Fry the strips
very briefly. They will turn and twist into gorgeous shapes.
Dry on kitchen paper.
The crisps will hold their shape for a few hours. **Serves 4**

Potatoes à la Boulangère

2 lbs (960g) old potatoes
1 large onion
1 grated carrot
1 teaspoon thyme
1 pint (500mls) chicken stock
Salt & pepper

Peel the potatoes and slice thickly.
Chop onions very finely and grate carrot.
Paint a two inch deep casserole dish with oil and place a layer of potatoes over the bottom, covered by a layer of onions, then a layer of grated carrots, salt, pepper and thyme, and finally another layer of potatoes.
Pour over chicken stock, brush the top with a little melted butter.
Cover the dish with a sheet of buttered greaseproof paper.
Put the dish on a hot baking tray and roast for about 50 minutes.

Serve the potatoes piping hot, in generous portions.
Garnish with sprigs of thyme.
Serves 4

Penne with Five cheeses

This is a very popular dish with young and old alike.
It came from an artist friend in Somerset, Mass.

1 pint of cream
Small can of tomatoes in their juice
4 ozs (120g) grated Parmesan cheese
4 ozs (120g) coarsely grated cheddar cheese
4 tablespoons of crumbled Gorgonzola cheese
2 tablespoons of Ricotta cheese
4 ozs (120g) fresh Mozzarella cheese, sliced
Half teaspoon salt
2 ozs (60g) butter
1lb (450g) penne

Pre-heat the oven to 450F/225C/gas mark 6.

Combine all the above ingredients except the penne and butter. Stir over a low heat until melted. This is your sauce. Boil a large saucepan of salted water. Drop the penne into the boiling water and parboil for 4 minutes. Drain. Add to the sauce. Toss to combine well. Place in a casserole dish. Dot with butter. Put into the oven and bake for about 7 to 10 minutes until bubbly and brown on the top. Serve with Sassaroli's bread (page 9) and a green salad. **Serves 4**

Linguine, Buccatini or Spaghetti with Basil Pesto Sauce

Basil and pesto have reached a near mythical status. How could any self-respecting cook or chef survive the summer without using that wonderful herb, basil? Use only young fresh basil as old stuff tastes dreadful. Use only fresh Parmesan cheese. Pesto (meaning paste in Italian) will last for weeks stored in a clean covered jar in the fridge. I find the best way of preventing a scum forming on top is to press a layer of cling film plastic on to the surface.
Pesto should be served only with dried pasta, not with the freshly made variety.

Basil Pesto Sauce

Pistachio nuts or walnuts can be used in place of the pinenuts and will make a subtle difference in taste. Experiment to discover your own favourite pesto.

3 cloves garlic
3 big bunches of basil
(enough to fill the bowl of the food processor)
1 small bunch parsley
Sea salt and pepper
1 pint (600mls) of best extra virgin olive oil
4ozs (120g) pinenuts
6ozs (180g) fresh Parmesan cheese, grated
2 tablespoons soft unsalted butter

Tear the leaves off the stalks of basil and parsley and put into the food processor with all the other ingredients except the cheese and butter.
Blend to a smooth purée cleaning down the sides of the bowl with a rubber spatula.
Beat in the butter and grated Parmesan cheese by hand.
Store pesto in a jar until ready to use.

Pasta

lb (450g) Spaghetti or Linguine or Buccatini
1.1/2 tablespoons salt
5 quarts(10L) water.

Bring the water to the boil and then add the salt and the pasta of your choice, stirring frequently to prevent the strands from sticking together. When cooked, drain, but not completely. This remaining water will facilitate the binding of the sauce with the pasta.
Add the pasta to the pesto sauce and toss well. Turn on to warmed plates and serve immediately. Grate a little extra Parmesan cheese on top. **Serves 4**

HIGH TEA

Poached Fillets of John Dory with a Citrus Sauce

Any other type of flat white fish besides John Dory can be used in this recipe. Get the fishmonger to fillet it for you.

4 fillets John Dory
4 tablespoons dry white wine
6 black peppercorns
1 bay leaf
1 small sliced onion

Citrus sauce:
Juice of 2 oranges
1 tablespoon caster sugar,
2 teaspoons cornflour
1 teaspoon water
1.1/2oz (45g) butter
Lemon to garnish

Place the fish in a single layer in a large frying pan with the wine, peppercorns, bay leaf and onion. Add enough water to barely cover the fish, poach over a medium heat until the fish is tender. Meanwhile, make the sauce.

Remove rind from one orange using a vegetable peeler. Cut rind into long thin strips and squeeze the juice from the 2 oranges. Place the sugar in a small saucepan and cook over a medium heat without stirring until the sugar is melted and golden in colour. Add the orange juice. Stir until this toffee mixture is melted. Blend the cornflour with cold water. Stir into sugar mixture.

Stir over a high heat until mixture boils and thickens. Remove from the heat. Add butter and rind and stir until butter is melted.

Place the cooked fish on hot plates.

Pour the sauce over. Garnish with a little bundle of the very finest slivers of lemon rind. **Serves 4**

HIGH TEA

Sautéed Potatoes with Balsamic Vinegar

This is a perfect recipe for using up left over cooked potatoes.

6 medium sized waxy potatoes (cooked)
Seasoned flour (with salt and pepper)
2 tablespoons groundnut oil
2 tablespoons balsamic vinegar

Scrub the potatoes and then cook them in their skins until they are just soft. Drain the potatoes and peel. Slice them into circles, half inch (1 cm) thick. Toss in the seasoned flour. Heat the oil in a frying pan. Put in the thick slices of potatoes. Toss in the oil until they are lightly browned and crispy.
Sprinkle with salt and balsamic vinegar. **Serves 4**

Herbed Mayonnaise

Just what the doctor ordered to lift cold meats to a higer plane!

1/2 pint (300mls) Mayonnaise
4 tablespoons (60mls) water
Salt and freshly ground pepper.
Generous bunch of fresh herbs,
such as lemon balm, parsley, basil and mint.
A few leaves of spinach (optional)

If you are using the spinach pull the leaves off the stems and dip briefly in boiling water.
Blend the mayonnaise with the herbs and spinach.
Slice cold meats attractively on a large platter.
Serve with herbed mayonnaise and perhaps a colourful salad of sliced orange with black olives. **Serves 4**

Ouine ʒan Oinnéaʀ
If you go without dinner,

beiʀc Oon csúipéaʀ!
You'll be able to feed two at suppertime!

Irish Proverb

Dinner

Dinner is a very special occasion and indeed, let there be no mistake, formal entertaining is a tricky business. The most important ingredients for a successful dinner party are the proper mix of guests and a cool hostess. You will always suceed if you have your preparation done beforehand. You should have a properly laid table, sparkling glasses, polished cutlery, fresh flowers and crisp linen. Strive to create a nice relaxed atmosphere with dimmed lights and glowing candles.

Music is a very essential ingredient and should be carefully chosen. A lot of Baroque music was written as background music and so is very suitable - Bach, Handel and Telemann. The latter's celebrated 'Tafelmusik ' was intended to be played while courtiers enjoyed a banquet and works very well for formal or informal gatherings. If you're not a classical fan, then try more contemporary options - Jon Mark's exquisite 'The Standing Stones of Callanish'; the guitar duet album 'Together and Together Again' by John Williams and Julian Bream; Brian Eno's 'Thursday Afternoon'; any album featuring Stephan Grappelli with Yehudi Menuhin e.g. 'Jealousy' or the Penguin Café Orchestra's 'Broadcasting from Home'.
Keep the volume low enough for comfortable conversation.

No matter how busy I am, I always inspect the tables before the guests make their appearance at dinner. I would like to think that when people arrive at the table , everything on it says 'I really do care about you and I am glad you came to dinner.'

Our evening in Ballymakeigh whizzes by in a blur of starters, soups, and sorbets until it is time for the real showpiece, the main course, which is always cooked, served and received with a kind of reverence! Finally the meal winds up in a haze of scrumptious desserts and gasps of delight. As the year goes round and the seasons change, our dinner menus vary accordingly. Our food complements the calendar during the year from New Year's Day to Christmas and back again.

St. Patrick's Day Dinner

St. Patrick's Day is a highlight of the Irish year, the feastday of our national saint. I always feel that spring has arrived when our avenue sports two long lines of dancing daffodils and little shamrocks appear on the gravel paths.

**A Trio of Cod with Buttered Mangetouts
and Warm Orange Segments
Poached Kassler Garnished with Black and White Puddings
Garlic Cabbage and Mushrooms
Chived Potatoes
Irish Lavender Honey Fudge Tart**

TRIO OF COD WITH BUTTERED MANGETOUT and WARM ORANGE SEGMENTS

4 pieces of cod, 3 ozs (90g) each, unskinned
2 teaspoons hazelnut oil
20 mangetout peas
12 segments of orange
3 dessertspoons of French dressing (page 23)
Sea salt

Heat the hazelnut oil in a non-stick frying pan. When the oil is hot, add the cod pieces, skin side down.   Cover the frying pan and cook for about five minutes turning the fish pieces twice. Wash the mangetout, place in a vegetable steamer with enough water to cover the bottom. Cook for one minute. Using a sharp knife, segment the orange. Warm the segments through in the oven or microwave.

Arrange the mangetouts evenly between each plate, placing the cooked cod on top. Divide the warmed orange segments, three to a plate, and finally drizzle French dressing around them.
Serves 4

Poached Kassler Garnished with Irish Black & White Pudding

Kassler is fresh loin of pork marinated with pepper, cloves and juniper berries and finally, oak smoked. It should be available from your butcher. I get it at O'Flynn's Butchers on Marlborough St., Cork. They will mail it to any place in the country. Tel: 021-275685/272195

**2.1/4 lbs (1kg) kassler
3 ozs (90g) sugar
1.1/2 ozs (45g) butter
2 ozs (60g) flour
4 thin slices each of Irish black and white pudding
Salt and pepper**

Place the kassler in a heavy bottomed saucepan and pour enough boiling water over it to cover.
Cook in placid, simmering water for about one hour, until ready.
Reserve cooking water for sauce.

Transfer the meat to a roasting tin. Sprinkle with sugar. Place meat in a hot oven for about five minutes, to caramelise.
Remove from the oven and then cover it with aluminium foil.
Rest in a warm place for about ten minutes. (the meat, not the cook!)
Meanwhile melt the butter, stir in the flour. Cook a little, and gradually add in the cooking liquid.
Add a little more flour if the sauce is too thin.
Taste, season with salt and pepper.

Fry slices of black and white pudding in the frying pan. Make sure that the slices are well done on each side and cooked through.
Arrange on a plate and then place pieces of sliced kassler beside the puddings. Pour sauce over.
Garnish with chopped parsley. **Serves 4**

DINNER

Garlic Cabbage and Mushrooms

6 ozs (180g) thickly sliced mushrooms
12 ozs (360g) shredded savoy cabbage
2 ozs (60g) bacon fat or butter
2 crushed cloves of garlic
2 tablespoons fresh lemon juice
Pinch salt and pepper
1 teaspoon caraway seeds (optional)

Slice mushrooms and shred cabbage.
Melt the bacon fat or butter in a heavy bottomed saucepan until foaming.
Add the mushrooms and garlic, fry for 3 minutes
Add the lemon juice, shredded cabbage, salt and pepper
The caraway seeds, though optional, add a certain piquancy.
Cook for about six minutes over a moderate heat, until the cabbage is tender.
Shake the pan to prevent the cabbage from sticking. Add a little water if it is inclined to stick.
Serve in a warmed serving bowl.
Serves 4

Chived Potatoes

4 large or 8 small potatoes
1 tablespoon chopped chives
Half a small carton of cream

Boil the potatoes and peel while hot. Place in an ovenproof dish.
Pour the cream mixed with chopped chives over the boiled potatoes and then reheat them in the microwave or oven. **Serves 4**

Irish Lavender-Honey Fudge Tart

This pastry is suitable for all sweet tarts. It is essential that all the ingredients and equipment are as cold as possible for pastry making.

Pastry:
6 ozs (180g) plain flour
Pinch of salt
1 oz (30g) icing sugar
3 ozs (90g) butter
Egg yolk beaten with 1 tablespoon cold water

Filling:
4 tablespoons pure Irish Lavender honey (or any pure honey)
4 tablespoons cornflour
1 teaspoon cocoa powder
Half pint (300 mls) milk

Icing:
1.1/2 tablespoons Armagnac, brandy or water.
3 ozs (90g) icing sugar
10 walnut halves.

8" (20cm) flan tin
Heat oven to 375°F/190°C/gas mark 5
Pre-heat baking sheet.

Sieve the flour, salt and icing sugar into a large mixing bowl.
Rub in the butter until you have a fine breadcrumbs mixture.
This can be done in the food processor. Then mix the water and egg yolk together. Make a well in the centre of the breadcrumbs mixture and add the egg mixture to it. Mix until the dough is holding well together.
Lightly flour the work surface and place the dough on to it.
(If you can do this on a marble slab, better still)
Knead lightly, wrap in cling film and chill.

This pastry should rest for an hour before cooking it. Before rolling it out, bring it back to room temperature.
Roll out pastry to fit an 8″ (20cm) buttered flan tin.

Run the rolling pin over the top of the flan tin. This will trim the pastry nicely.
Prick the base with a fork.
Line the flan with tinfoil. Fill with fiberglass beans.
Put on preheated baking sheet and bake for 20 minutes, then take out of the oven.
Take out beans and foil.
Put back in the oven to brown for about three minutes.
Remove, cool and if it is not to be used immediately store in an airtight tin.

Filling:
Melt the honey and the butter together. Mix the cocoa powder and cornflour to a paste with three tablespoons of cold milk taken from the half pint. Add the remaining milk to the honey mixture. Then bring to the boil stirring all the time. Add this to the cornflour paste. Allow to cool, pour into pastry case, scraping out the saucepan with a rubber spatula.
When cold, make the icing very simply by adding the Armagnac to the icing sugar.
Pour icing on to the flan and decorate with walnut halves.
Serve with softly whipped cream and sprigs of lavender, or with slices of banana and kiwi dipped in lemon juice and arranged in alternate circles.
Serves 4

Cooks Tip:
Roll a small piece of pastry into a ball, dip it in flour and use to press the pastry into the sides of the tin. Works a treat!

An té a ċuꞓ an ḃeaċa seo ꝺúinn,

May He who gave us this food

Ꞓo ꝺṫuꞓa sé an ḃeaċa síoraí ꝺúinn

Also give us the food of everlasting life.

Old Irish Blessing

Easter Menu

This time of special celebration warrants an extra special culinary treat

Cheese Soufflé with Smoked Salmon
Melon and Kiwi Sorbet
Lamb Goulash
Nutty Green Salad
Ginger Dressing
Chocolate Layer Pudding

Cheese Soufflé with Smoked Salmon

Cheese soufflé is my favourite starter to cook and serve, but I would recommend practising and making soufflés a few times before putting them on a dinner menu.
When I serve a soufflé for first course I always have a melon on standby just in case disaster strikes and my masterpiece does not rise as high as my hopes!!!

2 ozs (60g) breadcrumbs
12 ozs (360g) smoked salmon pieces
1.1/2 ozs (45g) butter
1 oz (30g) flour
Half pint (300mls) milk
Good pinch cayenne pepper
Half teaspoon curry powder
Pinch of grated nutmeg
Quarter teaspoon dried mustard
3 egg yolks and 4 egg whites (at room temperature)
3 ozs (90g) strong Cheddar cheese, grated
1 oz (30g) fresh Parmesan cheese
(do not even consider the powdered variety)
10 teaspoons chopped walnuts or hazelnuts for topping
Melted butter for buttering dishes

8 individual soufflé dishes
Preheat oven to 425°F/220°C/gas mark 7.

A soufflé mixture can be prepared and kept covered in the fridge but for only about 2 hours before cooking.

Butter the soufflé dishes really well, especially around
the rim, coat the insides with the breadcrumbs.

Put 1 oz (30g) smoked salmon into each soufflé dish.

Melt the butter in a saucepan, stir in the flour and cook until
foaming.

Cook over a low heat for 2 minutes.

Pour in the milk and whisk well.

Bring the mixture to the boil stirring continously.

Cook until sauce thickens.

Season with cayenne pepper, curry powder, nutmeg & mustard.

Take the saucepan from the heat.

Beat the egg yolks into the hot sauce one by one.

Stir in the grated cheese and test for seasoning.

In a spotlessly clean bowl beat the egg whites until they form a
shallow peak when the whisk is lifted.

They should be smooth and so stiff that they would not fall out if
the bowl was turned upside down.

Do not over-beat or they will become 'grainy'.

Add about a quarter of the egg whites into the cheese sauce and
stir until mixed.

Add this mixture to the remaining egg whites and fold together
as gently as possible. Spoon mixture into prepared soufflé dishes.
Sprinkle with chopped walnuts.

Place dishes on baking sheet and bake in preheated oven for 15
minutes approximately.

Do not over-cook the soufflés. They should be golden brown,
puffed and soft in the centre.

Set the dishes on plates and rush to the table with them, because
at this stage, the soufflé waits for no-one!

Serves 8

Cook's Tip
*I always rub the whisk and inside of the bowl with a slice of lemon
before whipping the egg whites*

Kiwi and Melon Sorbet

4 kiwis, peeled and chopped
1 honeydew melon, peeled, seeded and roughly chopped
Pinch of salt
2 tablespoons fresh lime juice.
4 fluid ozs (120mls) water
4 ozs (120g) sugar
4 tablespoons green Crème de Menthe.

Set freezer to lowest temperature.

Put kiwis, melon pieces and lime juice in a blender and process.
Put water and sugar into a small saucepan. Cook over a low
heat until the sugar is dissolved, about 2 minutes. Cool.
Add to the kiwi mixture. Blend well. Add the Crème de Menthe.
Put in ice-cream maker or freeze in the freezer. When it is frozen
reset freezer.
Remove from freezer and allow to thaw for 20 minutes before
serving.
Serve in attractive glasses decorated with lemon balm.
Serves 8 - 10

Cooks Tip
To extract more juice from a lemon or lime, pour boiling water over it
5 minutes before squeezing it, or put in microwave for 1 minute and
leave to cool a little before squeezing.

Lamb Goulash

For special occasions I like to use chump chops for this recipe. For an everyday menu I use neck of lamb. This dish benefits from being prepared the day before.

2 large onions (sliced thickly)
2 tablespoons rosemary flavoured oil
1 clove garlic
8 ozs (240g) leeks
1 tablespoon plain flour
1 tablespoon paprika
1 x 14 oz. (400g) tin of tomatoes
1/4 pint (150 mls) stock
Sprig of rosemary
1 teaspoon chopped ginger
2lbs (approx. 1 kg) neck of lamb, boned,
with excess fat removed, and cut into pieces
1 red or green pepper
4 tablespoons natural yoghurt
Some chopped parsley

Preheat the oven to 325°F/160C°/Gas mark 3
Preheat a baking sheet

Prepare leeks as on page 49
Slice onions into thick rings.
Heat the oil in a heavy frying pan. Lightly brown both sides of the meat pieces and place in a heavy bottomed casserole dish. Then add onions, garlic and leeks to the frying pan. Cook until onions turn a pale golden colour and then sprinkle in the flour and paprika. Stir to soak up the juices and then add tin of tomatoes, stock, seasoning and a sprig of rosemary and chopped ginger.
Bring to the boil and pour over the meat in the casserole. Cover the meat completely with the sauce and then cover the casserole dish with a tight fitting lid. Cook in the oven for up to two hours until the lamb is tender. Slice pepper into the casserole 30 minutes before the end of cooking, remembering to stir it well into the goulash. Just before serving skim the fat off the surface. Swirl in the natural yoghurt and chopped parsley and fresh mint. Serve with a nutty green salad. **Serves 4**

DINNER

Nutty Green Salad
with Ginger Dressing

4 good handfuls of fresh lettuce leaves, including cos, iceberg, rocket, radicchio, oakleaf
2 mangetout peas
4 ozs (120g) of broccoli divided into small florets
1/4 cucumber
4 ozs (120g) of Pecan nuts, chopped
Chopped fresh herbs,
A handful of Hawthorn leaves and buds.

Wash and dry lettuce leaves thoroughly, otherwise the dressing will not cling to the leaves. Place in an attractive salad bowl. Wash, dry and slice the mangetout. Add with broccoli to the bowl. Peel the cucumber, halve lengthwise, then quarter and chop into small dice. Put in a separate bowl with the salt and sugar to marinate. Add chopped nuts and herbs to the salad bowl. Add in the diced cucumber. Mix well.
Serves 4

Ginger Dressing:

2 teaspoons grated ginger
3 fluid ozs (75mls) lemon juice
6 fluid ozs (150mls) walnut oil
Half teaspoon dried mustard
Pepper
Pinch of sugar

Combine all the ingredients together in a screw top jar. Shake well. Add a small amount to the salad. It should only barely cover the leaves. Toss and serve immediately.

Chocolate Layer Pudding

For real holiday indulgence invest your calorie budget in a few spoonfuls of this delightful dessert.

4 rounded tablespoons of drinking chocolate
1 rounded tablespoon of coffee powder
4 ozs (120g) fresh white breadcrumbs
4 ozs (120g) demerara sugar
1/2 pint (300 mls) cream
Some fresh raspberries

Mix the chocolate, coffee, breadcrumbs and sugar together.
Whip the cream to form peaks and then spread alternate layers of chocolate mix and cream in a glass bowl, finishing with cream, or alternatively it can be made up by arranging the layers in very wide rimmed glasses.
This dessert must be refrigerated for at least ten hours.
Serve with fresh raspberries.
Serves 4

Romantic Dinner for Two

Passions increase with the heat of the Summer and those hot, heady days put us all in the mood for romance. The following menu will tantalize your taste buds and raise your sensations to a new height!! I will not, however accept responsibility for the consequences!

Crab Salad in Red Dresses on a Fresh Fruit and Herb Sauce
Sizzling Roast Duck with a Rich Wine Sauce
Parsleyed Butter Noodles
Poached Leeks with a Pink Peppercorn Vinaigrette
Oranges 'Out of the Fire'
Dessert Wine

Crab Salad in Red Dresses Served on a Fresh Fruit and Herb Sauce

2 ripe beef tomatoes
Pinch salt
A little sugar
Pinch cayenne pepper
6 ozs (175g) cooked crab meat
A dash of tabasco sauce
3 teaspoons mayonnaise

Cut the tops off the tomatoes. Using a teaspoon, scoop out the flesh and set aside. Remove the pips. Season the tomato shells with salt and sugar and cayenne pepper, then turn upside down to drain.
Combine the crab meat with the tabasco sauce, salt, pepper and mayonnaise. Adjust seasoning to taste.
Pile the crab mayonnaise into the tomato shells. Replace caps at an angle and garnish with parsley. **Serves 2**

Fresh Fruit and Herb Sauce

2 oranges
1 lemon
1 tablespoon honey
Fresh green herbs of your choice.
Half an avocado pear or piece of ripe melon

Juice the oranges and lemon.
Place with all the other ingredients in a blender and whizz.
Taste and season. It's as simple as that, your sauce is ready!
Serve the stuffed tomatoes on a pretty plate with the sauce poured around them. **Serves 2**

Sizzling Roast Duck with a Rich Wine Sauce

One 4 - 4.1/2 lb (2kg.) duck
Sea salt
Deep roasting tin.

About twelve hours before cooking, place the duck in the sink and pour a kettle of boiling water over it. Next, dry it thoroughly both inside and out and then leave it in a dry airy place for about 12 hours. This will help the skin to become dry and tight.

Pre-heat the oven to 375°F/180°C/gas mark 4.

Prick the skin all over with a pin or skewer to allow the fat to escape during cooking.
It is very important that you use a deep roasting tin for cooking the duck as a lot of fat will seep out during the cooking process and could spill over causing a nasty accident. Rub the duck all over with sea salt.
Place it on a wire rack in the oven for approximately 2 hours until cooked. Test by inserting a clean skewer into the thigh, and if the juices run clear the duck is cooked.
Take out of the oven and wait for about fifteen minutes before carving.
Serves 2

Rich Wine Sauce

1 pint (600mls) duck stock or beef stock
1/4 pint (150mls) red wine
2 tablespoons tomato sauce
Half teaspoon gravy browning
1 teaspoon arrowroot
Salt and pepper.

Put the stock, wine and tomato sauce into a saucepan.
Reduce the volume by half by boiling it rapidly.
For depth of colour add half a teaspoon of gravy browning.
Make a paste of the arrowroot by mixing with a little water.
Add to the gravy with a little water. Whisk well. Season with salt and pepper.
For a very shiny sauce add a knob of butter just before serving.

Cook's Tip
 Strain the duck fat and keep in a covered glass jar for other recipes.
It will roast potatoes beautifully, if used in place of your usual oil/fat.

Noodles with Parsleyed Butter

1 packet noodles
2 ozs (60g) butter
1 tablespoon chopped parsley

Cook noodles according to the directions on the packet. Melt the butter in a heavy bottomed saucepan. Be careful not to burn the butter. Drain the noodles, and toss them in the butter. Liberally sprinkle with parsley.   Serve immediately.

Poached Leeks with Pink Peppercorn Vinaigrette

6 baby leeks
Salt to taste
Fresh vegetable stock (pg. 21)

Vinaigrette:
1 tablespoon red wine vinegar
3 tablespoons extra virgin olive oil
2 tablespoons fresh lemon juice
2 tablespoons lightly crushed pink peppercorns
Freshly ground pepper

Prepare leeks as on page 49. Leave them whole.
Bring stock to the boil. Add leeks and salt to taste and cook for
about ten minutes until tender.
Remove from the liquid and drain well.
While the leeks are cooking, make the vinaigrette by whisking
the wine vinegar, oil, lemon juice, peppercorns and pepper
together.
At the last minute dress the leeks with the vinaigrette.
Serve warm.
Serves 2

Oranges 'Out of the Fire'

This is the perfect dessert to serve at a barbeque.

2 oranges
A sprinkling of sugar
2 tablespoons rum
4 squares of tinfoil

Oil the tinfoil and then peel the oranges removing all the white pith.
Slice them horizontally.
Sprinkle the sugar between the slices and then place each orange on a double layer of tinfoil.
Drizzle with the rum and then draw the foil up around the oranges and tie by scrunching the foil together.
At this stage of the evening you have two choices - put the oranges in a hot oven and heat them through, or a far more romantic idea would be, if the fire in the grate is at the smouldering stage and not very hot, just bury the 2 parcels in the ashes for about 10 minutes. Sit on a rug in front of the fire. Eat the oranges with a spoon.
Serves 2

Perfect with a glass of dessert wine, perhaps Muscat de Beumes-de-Venise.

Move over Adam and Eve!

Summer Dinner

Summer is a perfect time for entertaining guests and friends and nothing can be more enjoyable on long, hazy evenings than lingering over a dinner that takes in all the tastes of the season.

Pea Soup
Honey Glazed Roast Quail with Creamy Polenta
Sauteed Diced Vegetables with Raspberry Vinegar
Rich Orange Ice-cream with Grand Marnier Sauce

Pea Soup

Reserve the cooking stock from Kassler or boiled bacon for this deliciously simple recipe

2 pints (1L) of ham stock
1 X 14 oz (400g) tin of marrowfat peas
1 onion, chopped
A stick of celery, chopped
Bring all the ingredients to the boil. Then simmer for half an hour. Liquidize. Taste and season. If it is too thick, add a little water. Taste and season again. Serve garnished with cashew nuts and a swirl of cream
Serves 4

Honey Glazed Roast Quail with Creamy Polenta

Quail cooks so quickly that it could almost be classified as a convenience food

8 small quail
A little olive oil
2ozs (60g) butter
8 sprigs of thyme
4 teaspoons honey

Preheat oven to 400°F/300°C/gas mark 6

Quail will definitely benefit from being marinated overnight in olive oil and honey. If you do not have time to do this simply
heat the butter and olive oil in a large frying pan. Fry the quail a few at a time, in the hot oil, turning all the time until golden brown. Put a sprig of thyme in each carcass and tuck their wings behind them. Continue cooking by roasting them in a hot oven for about 15 - 20 minutes. Do not over cook.
Check for readiness by pulling away the leg. If it resists the bird is not cooked. Serve the quails on a bed of Polenta with sautéed diced vegetables and a raspberry vinegar. **Serves 4**

Polenta

1 lb (500g) Polenta (maize meal)
1 pint (500mls) good chicken stock
3 ozs (90g) fresh Parmesan cheese, grated
2 ozs (60g) butter
Salt and pepper
3 tablespoons tomato sauce

Add half the stock to the Polenta. Allow to soak.
Heat the rest of the stock. Pour over the soaked Polenta. Stir well. Cook over a low heat until cooked, about 25 minutes. Stir in the grated Parmesan , butter and tomato sauce. **Serves 4**

Sautéed Diced Vegetables with a Raspberry Vinegar

8 ozs (240g) diced carrots
8 ozs (240g) diced turnips
8 ozs (240g) diced courgettes
(Sprinkle the courgettes with a little salt and allow to stand for at
least 30 minutes before cooking)
2 ozs (60g) butter
2 tablespoons raspberry vinegar
Some finely chopped parsley
Salt and pepper

Prepare and dice the vegetables.
In a heavy bottomed saucepan, melt the butter and add the diced
carrots and turnips. Cook over a medium heat for five minutes.
Add the courgettes and raise the heat slightly. Stir the vegetables
and keep stirring until they are all cooked.
Stir in the raspberry vinegar and season with salt and pepper.
Cook for a further few minutes until the vinegar mixture
becomes syrupy. Put into a hot serving dish and garnish with
parsley. Serve immediately. **Serves 4**

As the sun goes down, dinner begins...........

Ballymakeigh Fillets of Pork with a Red Pepper Mousse (pg. 109)

Opposite right: The Master's Choice Menu (pg. 99) Clockwise from top right:
Cider Punch, Loin of Venison with selection of seasonal vegetables, Filo
Basket of Mushrooms & Pine Kernels on Mango Purée, Red Onion
Marmalade, Horseradish sauce and Redcurrant Jelly, Blackberried Pears, &
Creamed Potatoes, Runner Beans, and Tomato Concassé.

Pan-fried Scallops in a Noilly Prat Sauce (pg. 107)

Opposite right: Menu for the 2nd Millennium. From top: Rack of Ballyglassin Lamb with Leek and Watercress Purée, Rustic Salad of Roasted Red Onions, Cucumber and Cherry Tomatoes in a Herb Scented Cream, (pg. 114)

Sleepy Milk and Honey with Shortbread Biscuits (pg. 120)

Margaret's Christmas Cake (pg. 112)
Please Note: *Use a Size 9″ Round Tin.*

Tender loving care is the order of the day at Ballymakeigh.

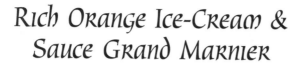

Rich Orange Ice-Cream & Sauce Grand Marnier

6 egg yolks
8 ozs (240g) caster sugar
2 oranges
2 tablespoons Grand Marnier
Half pint (300mls) cream

Set the freezer to the lowest possible setting

Whisk the egg yolks with sugar until white and fluffy. Grate the oranges and squeeze out the juice. Gradually beat in the grated rind and juice of the oranges. Add the Grand Marnier. Beat the cream until thick, but not too stiff and fold into the egg mixture. Put in a plastic covered container and freeze. Stir occasionally while freezing. Remove from freezer about 30 minutes before serving. Put it in the fridge to thaw.
Reset freezer to its normal setting when the ice cream is frozen.
Serves 6

Grand Marnier Sauce

2 tablespoons jelly marmalade
Quarter pint (150mls) orange juice
5 tablespoons Grand Marnier

Heat the marmalade until melted.
Then add the orange juice. Bring to the boil and set aside to cool.
In a separate saucepan heat the Grand Marnier. Tilt the saucepan to the side. Set the Grand Marnier alight with a match.
There will be a nice flame so keep your distance from the saucepan! It will burn off in seconds.
Add the Grand Marnier to the marmalade mixture. Do not re-boil.
Serve the ice cream in scoops. Pour a little of the sauce beside it.
Serves 6

No-Hassle Supper for 10

This dinner is a little bit more casual but no less delicious than all the others. All the recipes are for 10 people (multiply or divide according to numbers).

Nice bites
Cornucopias of Smoked Salmon
Pheasant Casserole served with Roast Quinces
Chicory Orange and Passion Fruit Salad
Tuiles of Cinnamon-Scented Brown Bread Ice-cream
with a snappy Ginger Sauce
Silky Irish Coffee
Afterthoughts - Bowls of Mints

Nice Bites

Hand around thin slices of baguettes spread with Pesto, (page 60) Parsnip crisps (page 58) and bowls of pitted olives. Olives are big business today. There are about 700 million productive olive trees in the world. The bulk of the harvest goes to making oil, the rest goes to the table. There are many varieties to choose from but for a cosy gathering I would choose two types, a brine cured green and an oil cured black.
Serve at room temperature.

Cornucopias of Smoked Salmon

If you love your friends enough, or you really want to impress them, make the cucumber cornucopias, otherwise serve the mousse on water biscuits

1 large cucumber
5 slices of smoked salmon
8 ozs (240g) cream cheese
Salt and pepper
2 tablespoons sultanas
1 teaspoon chopped dill or any other fresh herb
1 teaspoon horseradish sauce

First make the shapes for the cornucopias

Cut the cucumber widthwise into 3 1/2" (9cms) long pieces
Using a swivel potato peeler slice paper-thin flat rectangular slices off the cucumber. You should be able to get 30 - 40 pieces depending on the size of the cucumber. Leave them aside.

Cut the smoked salmon into small pieces.

Beat the cream cheese, horseradish sauce, herbs, salt and pepper together.
Add the chopped salmon and sultanas to this.
Make a tiny rolled case from one of the cucumber slices.
Fill it with 1 - 2 teaspoons of the mousse. Repeat using up all the cucumber slices and smoked salmon mousse.
Makes 40

Cook's tip:
Cucumber should always be sliced so thin that one could read the paper through it! You can do this quite successfully on the blades of a food processor.

DINNER

Pheasant Casserole with Baked Quince

If you wish you can replace the pheasant with chicken and still end up with a dazzling party piece. Pheasant is in season in Ireland from 1st October to 1st February. When buying a pheasant check that it has been hung for at least one week. Game from the wild does a lot more running around and exercising than their battery reared farmyard cousins so as a result their meat is tougher and needs longer hanging time.

5 jointed pheasants
4 tablespoons cooking oil

Marinade:
4 crushed juniper berries
4 sprigs thyme
2 sprigs of rosemary
2 sage leaves
2 teaspoons chopped parsley
2 bay leaves
2 small onions
3 celery sticks
3 carrots, peeled and quartered
2ozs (60g) fat pork or oil

1 pint (600 mls) red wine
1 tablespoon redcurrant jelly

1 X 240g tin of Chestnuts or frozen chestnuts

Pre-heat the oven to 375°F/190°C/gas mark 5

Roux:
2 ozs flour
2 ozs butter

To make the roux blend the flour and butter together and cook over a low heat for a few minutes.

To Marinate:
Place the pheasant pieces in a large bowl with all the marinade ingredients, except the red wine. Put the wine in a saucepan and bring to the boil. Allow to cool and then pour it over the pheasant pieces, leave to marinate overnight.
Take out the pheasant pieces and pat dry.
In a heavy casserole dish or large roasting tin heat the oil then add the pheasant pieces and brown all over.
Then add the marinade liquid to the pheasant in the casserole, cover and cook for about 45 minutes until the pheasant pieces are tender. Put in chestnuts 15 minutes before end of cooking.
Lift out the pheasant pieces and the vegetables and put in warm place covered with tinfoil.

Add one tablespoon of redcurrant jelly to the stock in the casserole. If it is too thin add a little roux, whisk it, boil it up and it will thicken very nicely.
Serve a breast and leg to each person.
Pour the sauce over the pheasant joints.
Garnish with chopped parsley and pitted grapes.

The vegetables which were marinated and cooked with the pheasant can be mashed coarsely, heated through and served in a separate dish.
Serves 10

Baked Quince

Quinces are a real treat. They are a very sour, rock hard, type of apple, yellow in colour, which changes to russet red on cooking. A good greengrocer will source them for you. Better still, grow your own. 'Champion', 'Meech's Prolific' or 'Vranja' are the varieties to get. In the absence of quince use cooking apples or pears or peaches. These fruit will not require as long cooking time as the quinces.

5 large quince, or whichever fruit you decide to use
2 teaspoons coriander powder
3 tablespoons caster sugar
3 tablespoons butter
10 shiny bay leaves

Cut the fruit in half horizontally. Take out the core.
Cut a thin slice off the bottom of the fruit so they will sit upright.
Put the fruit halves, centre half up, into a shallow baking dish packing them close together.
Sprinkle with sugar and coriander.
Dot each one with butter.
Put a few spoons of water around the fruit.
Keep dish filled with water and baste regularly.
Bake until fruit is cooked - quince about 1 hour, the other fruit would only take about 20 - 25 minutes.
Serve with shiny bay leaves stuck in them - not to be eaten!
Serves 10

Cook's Tip:
Quinces will emit a beautiful scent in a room if left sitting on the window sill or table.

DINNER

Chicory, Orange and Passion Fruit Salad

This dramatic looking salad will be a perfect contrast to the wine colour of the casseroled pheasant and russet colour of the quince.

2 heads of chicory
4 oranges
3 passionfruit

French dressing (Page 23)

Divide the heads of chicory into leaves (keeping them intact).
Peel and segment oranges saving any juice to add to French dressing.
Halve the passionfruit. Scoop out seeds.
Arrange the chicory leaves on a large plate. Place the orange segments on top.
Scatter the passion fruit seeds over the salad, and drizzle lightly with French dressing.
Serves 10

The Magic Tuile

Tuiles are wafer thin, elegant little biscuits to serve with desserts or on their own with tea or coffee. They are so easy to make that I find it hard to believe that it took me hours to master them. In fact, I started making my first tuile one evening at 4 o'clock. After rejecting 100s of them, I finally figured out how to do them by 1 a.m. the following morning!
The secret of successful tuiles lies in using the correct ingredients, taking them off the tins when they are just browning and then storing them in an airtight tin immediately.
Recipe overleaf

Tuiles of Cinnamon-Scented Brown Bread Ice-Cream with a Snappy Ginger Sauce

Tuiles
3 ozs (90g) icing sugar
2 ozs (60g) butter
2 egg whites
2 ozs (60g) flour

2 lightly buttered Swiss roll tins

Preheat oven to 400°F/200°C/gas mark 6.

Beat the sugar and the butter together.
Add the egg whites and the flour to make a batter.
Put a teaspoon of the mixture on tin, and spread it evenly. You should fit about 3 tuiles on each tin. Place in the oven, watch carefully as they will only take two minutes to cook.
Have upturned cream or yoghurt cartons ready. As soon as the tuiles are lightly browned take them from the oven, lift each tuile off the tin with a knife and place on top of an upturned cream carton. Mould into a nice shape. You can also roll them up into cigar shapes. Store when cool, in an airtight container.
Serves 10

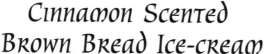

Cinnamon Scented Brown Bread Ice-cream

6 ozs (180g) stale breadcrumbs made from wholemeal
brown bread
2.1/2 ozs (75g) butter
3 ozs (90g) brown sugar
8 eggs (separated)
8 ozs (240g) caster sugar
1 teaspoon cinnamon
1 pinch salt
1 pint (600mls) cream

Set the freezer to its lowest temperature.
Melt the butter in a frying pan. Add the crumbs and toss and turn
over a moderate heat. Add the sugar and stir until the crumbs are
brown and caramelised. A little patience is required here, but the
lovely, crunchy result is well worth the effort. Allow to cool.
Carefully separate eggs and place the whites in a large, spotlessly
clean bowl. Add the salt.
Whip the egg whites until stiff and then add caster sugar, one
teaspoonful at a time. Beat well. Whisk the egg yolks until well
blended. Whip the cream with the cinnamon until it forms soft
peaks, and remember that over-beating will destroy the consistency.
Fold the egg yolk mixture into the meringue mixture. Fold whipped
cream into this mixture with the breadcrumbs. Use a metal spoon for
all the folding process, working quickly and efficiently so as to
maximize the air circulation within the mixture.
Put into a covered plastic container and place in freezer at its lowest
temperature for two hours. Remove and stir with a metal spoon.
Put back in freezer. Remove one hour before serving and put it in
the fridge to soften. When the ice-cream is frozen, re-set freezer to
normal temperature. **Serves 10**

Cook's tip:
*To separate eggs, break egg into saucer. Place a drinking glass over
the yolk and the white will flow away from it.*

Snappy Ginger Sauce

4 ozs (120g) soft brown sugar
8 ozs (240mls) water
4 tablespoons preserved ginger
1 tablespoon lemon juice

This ginger sauce is made by heating the sugar and water in a saucepan, stirring all the while until the sugar is dissolved. Bring to the boil until the mixture thickens and then stir in the ginger and the lemon juice.
Serves 10

Cook's tip:
Store fresh ginger indefinitely by peeling and cutting it into small chunks, place in a glass jar, cover with dry sherry, and store in the fridge.

'One for the Road' - A Silky Irish Coffee

4 generous measures of Irish whiskey
12 fl. ozs (240mls) strong black coffee
8oz (240g) best quality vanilla ice-cream
A little icing sugar to taste

Whizz all the ingredients together in the food processor.
Pour into chilled cups or mugs and serve at once.
Whether you are making hot or cold Irish coffees, instant coffee works best.
Serves 4

The Master's Choice

This menu includes some of nature's greatest delicacies.

Cider Punch
Filo Baskets of Mushrooms and Pine Kernels
on a Mango Purée
Loin of Venison in its own Juices
Red Onion Marmalade
Creamed Potatoes with Runner Beans and Tomato Concassé
Blushing Blackberried Pears

Cider Punch

1 flagon of dry or medium dry cider
1 glass of dark rum
1 orange, peeled and sliced
1 apple, cored and sliced
Pinch of freshly grated nutmeg
2 cinnamon sticks
Sugar to taste

Mix all the ingredients together and heat very gently before serving.
Serve in a large pre-heated punch bowl. Ladle into wine glasses.
Try to give everyone a slice of orange and a slice of apple.

Filo Baskets of Mushrooms and Pine Kernels on a Mango Base

8 sheets filo pastry
A little melted butter
1 lb (450g) mushrooms (wild if possible)
1 onion
1 teaspoon anchovy essence
2 slices of pineapple
4 ozs (120g) pine kernels
1 tablespoon soy sauce
1 tablespoon oil
1 oz (30g) unsalted butter
A little lemon juice
Mango purée
Some sprigs of dill and sliced cucumber for garnish
2 dessertspoons crème fraîche

4 ramekin dishes
Set oven to 350°F/160C°/gas mark 3. Heat baking sheet in oven.

Keep filo pastry covered while handling, otherwise it will dry out. Cut it into 12 six inch squares. Stack them on top of each other and cover with a cloth.
Paint the ramekin dishes generously with melted butter.
Paint one piece of filo with melted butter.
Arrange in ramekin dish. Repeat with next 2 pieces of filo arranging them in the ramekin dish at slight angles.
Make a slit through the base of the pastry. Repeat the same procedure with the other 3 dishes. Bake for about 15 minutes watching them very carefully, as they will burn in a flash. When they are nice and crispy remove from oven. Take the cases out of the ramekin dishes. Cool on a wire tray. They will last for a few days in an airtight tin.

Clean mushrooms with a piece of damp kitchen paper.
Slice thickly.
Peel and chop the onion finely.
Melt the butter and oil.
Add onions, cover and cook.
When cooked remove to a bowl.

Heat the oil and the butter again until very hot.
Add the mushrooms, cook over a high heat. When cooked add a squeeze of lemon juice, soy sauce, anchovy essence, salt and pepper.

Add in the onions, pine kernels and chopped pineapples.
Add in 2 dessertspoons of crème fraîche. Taste and season.
Slice cucumber very thinly. Divide into quarters.
Put the mango purée in a saucepan to heat.
If you wish you can thicken it with 1 teaspoon of arrowroot.
Add the arrowroot dissolved in 1 teaspoon of purée. Whisk like mad!

Reheat the cases in oven. Reheat the mushroom mixture.
Arrange quarters of cucumber around the edge of the plates.
Pour mango purée on to the plates. Put filo case off centre on the plate. Fill with mushroom filling. Garnish with sprig of fennel.
Serves 4

Loin of Venison in its Own Juices

2.1/2lbs (1 kg) Loin of Venison
Olive Oil
Black pepper

Preheat oven to 400°F/200°C/gas mark 6.

Venison definitely benefits from being marinated overnight - see pages 22 and 23 for recipes. After marinating, pat dry, and dust with black pepper.

Heat oil in a heavy frying pan, and seal the venison on all sides for a few minutes. Put into a hot oven for about 20 minutes to cook. Remove from oven. Cover loosely with tinfoil and rest it for 10 minutes before carving.

Serves 4

Red Onion Marmalade

Red Onion Marmalade is delicious either hot or cold with any meat dish. It is especially good with quail, lamb or beef.

1.1/2lbs (700g) red onions
2 tablespoons groundnut oil
Enough red wine to barely cover the onions
4 fluid ozs. (150mls) vinegar
2 tablespoons grenadine syrup
Salt and pepper
3 ozs (90g) sugar

Slice the onions very thinly then heat the oil.
Toss the onions in the hot oil, add the rest of the ingredients.
Allow to soften, cook over a medium heat until all the liquid is absorbed.
Season to taste - it should be both sweet and sour.
Serves 4

Creamed Potatoes with Runner Beans and Tomato Concassé

Concassé is a French term meaning peeled and roughly chopped.

8 good sized old potatoes
Half pint (300mls) milk
2 ozs (60g) butter
Salt and white pepper

8 ozs (240g) runner beans
1 tomato

Wash, scrub and boil potatoes. Peel while hot.
Boil milk. Add to the potatoes
Add the cold butter, salt and pepper. Mash very well.
Taste. Add more salt, pepper or butter if necessary.

Meanwhile, cook the runner beans in a little boiling water for a few minutes. Toss in melted butter.
Chop the tomatoes into fine dice.
Take a large serving plate.
Pipe the potatoes to form a base. Then pipe rosettes of potatoes around the edge. Fill with the runner beans and tomatoes.
Flash under a hot grill just before serving. **Serves 4**

Blushing Blackberried Pears

Blackberries must not be gathered after October 11th, according to an old country tradition. October 11th was the old Michaelmas Day before the calendar changes of 1752. It was said to be on this day that Satan was thrown out of Heaven by the Archangel Michael. He fell into a bramble bush and now every year he takes his revenge by piddling on the blackberry plant on the anniversary of his disgrace! Not only will the berries taste sour but they will bring you bad luck! Hence the saying, "October blackberries are the Devil's".....Would I lie to you?

Of course, blackberries freeze perfectly so we can have them all year round.

The best variety of pear to use is William. or Conference would be the next choice.

6 firm ripe dessert pears
1 lb (480g) blackberries
Juice of half a lemon
2 ozs (60g) sugar
Half a cinnamon stick
1 oz (30g) whole cloves
Half teaspoon ginger
A few sweet geranium leaves
Half pint (300 mls) water
6ozs (180g) hazelnuts

You will need a saucepan that can accommodate the pears lying down.

Put about two thirds of the blackberries with the water, sugar, lemon juice, spices and geranium leaves into a heavy bottomed saucepan.

Bring to simmering point and then quickly peel the
pears, keeping each one intact and retaining the stalks.
Place the pears in the blackberry purée and poach gently over
a low heat.
Turn them a few times until they are evenly cooked and tender.
Lift out the pears and stand each one on a wide white soup
plate.
Taste the purée and add sugar if required.
Sieve the purée and return to the saucepan, heat it through with
the remaining blackberries.
Spoon the berries around the pears, pouring the sauce on top.
Scatter some hazelnuts around the finished dessert and serve
with thick natural yoghurt or whipped cream.
Serves 4

Cook's tip:
If you have some blackberry purée left, mix with a bottle of soda water
for a refreshing drink.

Christmas Menu

Christmas is a time of celebrating and feasting. We can deviate slightly from the traditional fare while still including some of the usual seasonal delights.

Pan Fried Scallops served in a Noilly Prat Sauce
Sparkling Cranberry and Vodka Sorbet
Ballymakeigh Fillets of Pork with a Red Pepper Mousse
Roast Potatoes
Mangetout Stars
Spicy Fruit Salad with Oomph!
Margaret's Christmas Cake

Pan Fried Scallops
served in a Noilly Prat Sauce

Scallops are very easy to cook and require the minimum of preparation. Just make sure you buy from a reliable fishmonger and that the fish smells very fresh. Any slight smell of ammonia is a sure tell-tale sign of bad fish. Do not even consider frozen scallops. You will end up with a big pool of expensive water and stringy fish!

Allow 3 scallops per person

2 ozs (60g) approx. of butter
2 tablespoons grainy mustard

For the sauce:
2 ozs (60g) butter
1 onion peeled and chopped finely
5 fl ozs (150mls) Noilly Prat
4 tablespoons water or fish stock
3 tablespoons cream
Squeeze of lemon juice.

You could make the sauce first and keep it in a thermos flask.

To make the sauce:
Melt the butter Add finely chopped onions. Fry them gently until soft but not browned. Add the Noilly Prat. Boil until its volume is reduced by half. Add the water or stock followed by the cream. Put on a low heat. Reduce a little further. Add some lemon juice, salt and pepper. For extra shine in the sauce beat in a knob of butter just before serving.

To cook the scallops:
Take them out of their shells. Rinse under a cold tap. Pat dry. Put the butter and mustard into a frying pan. Melt over a low heat. When hot, add the scallops.
Fry for about 3 minutes on each side until cooked.
Serve on hot plates with the sauce spooned around them.
Garnish with flat parsley or dill. **Serves 4**

DINNER

Sparkling Cranberry and Vodka Sorbet

On the evenings I serve dinner to my guests, and also for any special dinner parties for ourselves, I always serve a sorbet between starter and main course. I use the basic recipe outlined below for all of them - I just change the fruit purée and flavourings.

Makes 2 pints (1.2 litres)
1 pint (600mls) water
8ozs (240g) sugar
1 pint (600 mls) cranberry purée
1 capful of Vodka
1 egg white

Turn freezer to the lowest setting.

Place water and sugar together in a small saucepan.
Heat gently until the sugar dissolves. Bring to the boil. Boil steadily for 8 minutes. Leave it to get cold.
Add the fruit purée and Vodka to the syrup. Mix well. At this stage place in an ice-cream maker or put in a plastic covered container. Freeze in the freezer until very mushy. Take out of the freezer and process in the food processor or blender.
Whip the egg white. Fold into the sorbet gently. Freeze.
When frozen re-set freezer to proper setting.
Take out of freezer half an hour before serving and leave it in the fridge to soften a little.
Scoop it into pretty glasses and serve.
For speed on Christmas Day put the sorbet into the individual glasses beforehand and freeze.
Take out about 10 minutes prior to serving. **Serves 10**

Cook's tip:
Ice-cream and sorbets will freeze faster if put in stainless steel container in the freezer.

DINNER

Ballymakeigh Fillets of Pork with a Red Pepper Mousse

You can prepare this dish on Christmas Eve.

3 fillets of pork (pork steaks)
15 long and generous back rashers

Stuffing

1 medium onion
5 small cloves of garlic
2 large red peppers
5 tablespoons cooking oil
1 tablespoon mango chutney
Half teaspoon English mustard
2 ozs (60g) pinenuts (optional)
Half teaspoon caraway seeds (optional)
Pinch of pepper (no salt)

First make the stuffing:
Chop onion finely. Crush the garlic. Quarter, de-seed and chop red peppers.
In a heavy bottomed saucepan heat the oil. Add the garlic and onion and cook until soft. Then add the diced red peppers and cook for a further 5 minutes.
Add the nuts, caraway seeds, mango chutney and mustard. Mix well together.

It is important to allow the stuffing to cool before stuffing the pork.

continued overleaf.....

Ballymakeigh Fillets of Pork with Red Pepper Mousse continued

Preheat oven to 350°F/180°C/gas mark 4.

Take the 3 fillets of pork, cut each one in two lengthways. You will now have 6 long strips of pork.
Take a sheet of tinfoil, paint it with oil.

Lay the rashers side by side on the foil.
Lay 3 pork strips on top.
Spread stuffing along the top.
Lay the other 3 pork strips on top of the stuffing.
Enclose the pork with the rashers then draw the foil around the 'joint' and secure firmly. The rashers will act as an overcoat for the pork and keep it moist.
Put it in the roasting tin. Place in the oven and cook for one and three quarter hours. Turn the joint a few times during cooking to ensure even cooking throughout.
Take it out of the oven and leave to rest for 10 minutes before carving.
Make a slit in the tinfoil. Drain any juice into a saucepan, add the stock and red wine, reduce down a little. Add cream. Boil. If it is too thin, add a teaspoon of arrowroot. Whisk.
Carve the meat.
Serve on a cushion of apple sauce. (see next page) Garnish with slices of oranges, black grapes and parsley, with the gravy served 'on the side'.
Serves 6

Apple Sauce

Wash and core 4 apples.
Put into the hot oven on a baking dish with a little water, while
the meat is cooking.
They will be soft and mushy after about 30 minutes.
Take out of the oven. Allow to go cold.
Take the pulp out of the skin. Mix in a little sugar with it to taste
- there it is, a lovely, rich apple sauce.

Gingered Roast Potatoes

Good quality, even sized old potatoes
1 knob of butter
2 ozs (60g) oil
4 fl.ozs (80 mls) herbed stir-fry oil
1 teaspoon grated ginger
Sesame seeds

Wash and peel the potatoes.
Melt the butter and oil in microwave or saucepan
Add stir-fry oil, and grated ginger.
Toss potatoes in this and coat well.
Sprinkle with sesame seeds.
Place in baking dish and cook in the oven for 1 hour, turning
them at least twice during cooking.

Mangetout Stars

Allow 4 mangetout peas per person.
Make a slit in one and thread the other through it to form an 'X'
shaped star. Continue until you have 4 stars made. Cook in
boiling water for 2 minutes or cook in the microwave for 1
minute.
When serving the pork, place a star on each plate.

DINNER

Hot Fruit Salad with Oomph!

2 ozs (60g) butter
Quarter teaspoon of ground mixed spice
1 teaspoon of mild curry powder (This is not a misprint!)
15 oz can (425g) of pineapple cubes in its natural syrup, drained.
(Retain the juice for other uses).
8 oz can of peaches, in its natural juices, also drained
2 eating apples, cored and sliced
2 bananas, sliced
4 ozs (120g) grapes
2 ozs (60g) sultanas

Melt the butter in a large frying pan. Add the mixed spice and curry powder. Cook over a low heat for 2 or 3 minutes stirring frequently. Add all the fruit and toss well in the spicy butter. Continue cooking and tossing the fruit for 5 minutes until heated through. Add some of the reserved juices to moisten the fruit. Serve piping hot with whipped cream, crème fraîche or your favourite ice-cream. Decorate with sweet geranium leaves. **Serves 6**

Margaret's Christmas Cake

November 20th is the traditional day to start making Christmas puddings and cakes.
You need to have all your ingredients at room temperature especially eggs.
12 ozs (360g) softened unsalted butter
12 ozs (360g) caster sugar
16 ozs (480g) flour
Half teaspoon cinnamon
Half teaspoon mixed spice
Half teaspoon salt
6 large eggs

1 small tin of strawberries, drained
(reserve syrup for a fresh fruit salad)
Juice and grated rind of 1 orange

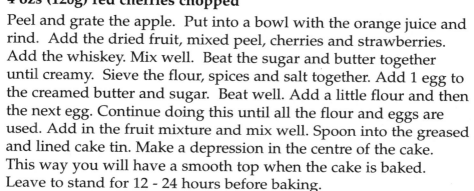

1 cooking apple
2 lbs (960g) of dried fruit
(A mixture of sultanas, raisins and currants)
3 tablespoons Irish whiskey
2 tablespoons golden syrup
4 ozs (120g) mixed peel
4 ozs (120g) red cherries chopped

Peel and grate the apple. Put into a bowl with the orange juice and rind. Add the dried fruit, mixed peel, cherries and strawberries. Add the whiskey. Mix well. Beat the sugar and butter together until creamy. Sieve the flour, spices and salt together. Add 1 egg to the creamed butter and sugar. Beat well. Add a little flour and then the next egg. Continue doing this until all the flour and eggs are used. Add in the fruit mixture and mix well. Spoon into the greased and lined cake tin. Make a depression in the centre of the cake. This way you will have a smooth top when the cake is baked. Leave to stand for 12 - 24 hours before baking.

Preheat oven to 350°F/180°C/gas mark 4.

Put the cake into the oven, close the oven door gently. Leave at this temperature for one and a half hours. Then lower temperature to 325°F/170°C.gas mark 3 for 1 hour, then to 275°F/140°C/mark 1 for 1 hour. Test for readiness by inserting a skewer in the cake. If it comes out clean the cake is ready, otherwise cook for a little while longer testing all the time.

Turn off oven. Leave the cake in the tin to cool completely, then remove it.

Wrap in greaseproof paper and store in a cool, dry place.

The topping can be put on two weeks before Christmas.

To decorate cake:

Brush top with warm sieved marmalade. Work fast as the marmalade cools and thickens very quickly. It acts as a glue for the nuts and fruit. Choose your own selection of preserved fruit and nuts of different sizes and shapes. I used red, green and yellow cherries, crystallized orange peel, brazil nuts, hazel nuts, pecans, walnuts, almonds and pistachios. It is not necessary to blanch and peel all the nuts but do blanch some as it gives you more colour. Now arrange the fruit and nuts in a pleasing pattern placing them very close together. Don't allow any of the cake to show through. You can work in spirals, circles, quarters or, as I did, in stripes. Warm up some more sieved marmalade and brush it on as a glaze.

Menu for the Second Millennium

This is a time when we must bridge the gap between past and future, bringing our traditional tastes into the next millennium while at the same time creating food for the future. Some of these recipes are a 90s creation which brought me much luck , when I won the Calor National Housewife of the Year award, and I hope they will also bring luck to future generations. Much of this food has endured the test of time for generations, most notably the marrowfat peas which have been cultivated since 5,000 B.C.

Warm Smoked Irish Salmon with Pear and Mango
Pomegranate Rose Sorbet
Rack of Ballyglassin Lamb with Leek and Watercress Purée
Cucumber and Cherry Tomatoes in a Herb Scented Cream
Marrowfat peas with Wild Rice
Rustic Salad of Roasted Red Onions,
Salad Leaves and Knockalara Cheese
Chilled Dessert Wine with Black Grapes

Warm Smoked Irish Salmon with Pear and Mango

8 slices of smoked salmon
2 ozs (60g) unsalted butter
Cubed flesh of a ripe mango
2 large ripe pears, preferably William or Conference
1 tablespoon lemon juice
Tiny pinch of chilli powder
4 large sprigs of fennel

First prepare the fruit.
Peel, halve and core the pears, chop into cubes.
Toss in lemon juice.
Pile the cubed mango on top of the pear cubes.
Dust lightly with chilli powder.
Divide the fruit between 4 plates.

In a large frying pan melt the butter. Add the salmon slices and
just barely heat them through. Remove and drape 2 pieces of
smoked salmon over each mound of fruit.
Garnish with sprigs of fennel.
Serves 4

Pomegranate Rose Sorbet

12 ozs (360g) sugar
Three quarters of a pint (400 mls) of water
1 tablespoon gelatine
2 pomegranates
2 teaspoons rosewater
1 egg white

Set the freezer to lowest temperature.
Put sugar and water into a saucepan. Heat gently, stir until sugar
dissolves. Then bring to the boil for 8 minutes. Cool.
Put 3 tablespoons of water into a small bowl. Shake the gelatine
into the water. Stand the bowl in a small saucepan of water. Heat
the water. The gelatine will dissolve. Take the bowl out of the
saucepan. Add a little of the syrup to it. Then add the gelatine
substance to the syrup, whisking well. Roll the pomegranates on
a hard surface to loosen the seeds. Halve the fruits.
Scoop the pulp into the bowl of the food processor. Using the
plastic blade, whizz them around. Put this mixture into a sieve
and push through as much of the juice as possible into the syrup.
Add in the rose water. Reserve a few seeds for decoration.

Put into a covered container.
Freeze until it becomes mushy.
Take out of the freezer and whizz it again in the food processor
or blender.
Whip egg white.
Fold it into the sorbet very gently. Freeze until needed.
Re-set freezer when the sorbet is frozen.
Take out half an hour before serving and leave in trhe fridge to
soften.
Serves 4

For the night that's in it, serve in wide rimmed champagne glasses.
Scatter some pomegranate seeds on top. Decorate with lemon balm.

DINNER

Rack of Ballyglassin Lamb with Leek and Watercress Purée

2lb (approx. 1kg) rack of lamb, usually there are 6 chops in
each one
4 bay leaves
Salt and freshly milled black pepper
1 lb (480g) leeks (washed and trimmed as on page 49)
3 ozs (90g) butter
5 fl. ozs (150mls) cream
Bunch of watercress, washed, drained and chopped.

Marinate lamb overnight if possible (see pages 22 & 23). Trim
any surplus fat from the lamb and tuck half a bay leaf between
the chops where the butcher has chined it. Lightly season the
meat, place in a roasting pan and roast in a moderate oven,
375°F/190°C/gas mark 5 for 45-60 minutes according to how
pink you prefer the meat. Remove from the oven and keep in a
warm place for 15 minutes for the juices to disperse through the
meat. Cover with tinfoil.
Slice the leeks finely and cook in 2ozs of the butter with a little
salt for 8-10 minutes until tender, stirring now and again. There
should be very little liquid left. If necessary raise the heat to
evaporate it.
Purée the leeks with the cream in a food processor or blender,
the mixture should be smooth but thick.
Melt the remaining butter and add the watercress. Stir over a
moderate heat for 1-2 minutes until the watercress has collapsed
but is still bright green. Stir into the leek purée, and serve with
the lamb.
Serves 4.

Cook's Tip
*The Leek and Watercress Purée can be frozen for 2-4 weeks. Thaw and
re-heat, covered, in a hot oven.*

DINNER

Cucumber and Cherry Tomatoes in Herb Scented Cream

The colour in this simple dish is a knockout!

Half pint (300mls) cream
Fresh herbs, crushed (dill, tarragon and basil)
1 cucumber
1 lb (480g) cherry tomatoes
Half oz (15g) butter
1 teaspoon sugar
Pinch salt
Squeeze of lemon juice

Stir the crushed herbs into the cream and leave to infuse.
Peel, halve and seed the cucumber. Cut the cucumber flesh into
pieces the size of the tomatoes. Put the cucumber into a bowl with
the salt and sugar and leave for 20 minutes. Then drain off the liquid
and dry the cucumber pieces. Make a cross on top of each tomato.
Put into a bowl. Pour boiling water over them, count to 10 - the skins
will peel off very easily. Fry the cucumber in hot butter for two
minutes, then add the tomatoes and cook for a further two minutes
and then put in the cream. Add the pepper, salt and lemon juice to
cook for a short while until lovely and creamy. Sprinkle in the fresh
herbs. **Serves 4**

Wild Rice with Marrowfat Peas

8oz (250g) marrowfat peas
8oz (250g) wild rice
1oz (30g) melted butter
Salt pepper, and sugar to taste
pinch of nutmeg

Rinse peas and soak overnight in cold water. Drain well. Cook
according to instructions. Drain and reserve. Cook rice in a wide
saucepan, following instructions. When cooked, add to peas, toss
in melted butter and add salt, pepper, sugar and nutmeg to taste.
Serves 4

DINNER

Rustic Salad of Roasted Red Onions, Salad Leaves & Knockalara Cheese

4 medium sized red onions
Extra virgin olive oil
4 handfuls of different salad leaves
(i.e. Oakleaf, Iceberg Lettuce, Raddichio, Sorrel, Rocket or Frisée)

Dressing
2 - 3 drops sesame oil
Lemon juice to taste
White wine to taste
A pinch of brown sugar
Half teaspoon mustard powder
Salt and pepper
Cubes of Knockalara Cheese
Black olives

Peel and slice red onions into 2 cm. sections and arrange these in a single layer on a lightly oiled baking sheet.
Brush the surfaces of each slice with olive oil. Season with salt and pepper. Bake in a hot oven for about 20 minutes. Remove. Prepare, wash and dry all the salad leaves thoroughly. At the last minute, whisk together all dressing ingredients and toss the salad leaves in it. They should be only barely coated with the oil. Arrange the salad leaves attractively in a salad bowl. Then add the roasted onions and cubes of Knockalara cheese. **Serves 4.**

Chilled Dessert Wine with Black Grapes

Serve each glass of chilled dessert wine with 12 grapes on a crisp white doyley. Eat at midnight! Each grape represents a month of the year. Reminisce and ponder the year ahead............!

Midnight Snacks

Since we are a land of milk and honey, what better way to finish the day than with a mug of Sleepy Milk and Honey, with Shortbread Biscuits or Toasted Barm Brack and Apple.

Sleepy Milk and Honey

This is a great cure for the insomniac

Measure the amount of milk needed, and pour into a heavy bottomed saucepan. Bring almost to the boil and pour immediately into mugs already prepared with a round teaspoon of honey in each. Stir and sip...............

ʒo méa�oaí Ɔia bainne
May God increase this milk

aʒus a máiꞇꞃeaċ ċuʒaiḃ
and it's motherly source to you

Old Irish Blessing

LATER...

Shortbread Biscuits

6 ozs (180g) flour
4 ozs (120g) butter (softened, preferably unsalted)
2 ozs (60g) caster sugar

Heat oven to 350ºF/180ºC, gas mark 4.
Put all the ingredients into the food processor and when mixed
take out and knead the mixture. Roll it out nice and thick, cut
into shapes and put in the oven for about 10 minutes. Don't let
them get coloured or they will be hard and bitter. Take them out
of the oven when still very soft and they will harden up after-
wards. Dust with icing sugar.
Makes approximately 20 biscuits

Toasted Barm Brack and Apple

2 dessert apples
1 tablespoon lemon juice
4 thick slices of barm brack, with the usual Hallowe'en treats
such as the ring, the stick, piece of cloth, etc.
Knob of butter
2 tablespoons of pineapple and melon jam or apricot jam
1 teaspoon powdered cinnamon

Peel, core and slice apples into rings. Toss well in lemon juice.
Under the grill toast the slices of barm brack on one side only.
Turn over and butter the other side.

Heat the jam until melted. Put the apple slices on the barm
brack slices. Brush with the melted jam. Sprinkle with cinnamon.
Grill until brown and bubbling.

Serve with whipped cream or crème fraîche (optional)
Serves 4

Index

Index

Index

Index

Measurement Conversions

Solid Measures

Imperial..............to...................Metric	Imperial...............to................American
1/2 oz....................................15g	
	Butter
1 oz................................. 30g	1 oz................................. 2 Tablespoons
	8 oz....................................... 1 cup
2 oz 60g	
	Flour
4 oz /1/4 lb..............................120g	1 oz.................................1/4 cup
	8 oz....................................... 2 cups
8 oz / 1/2 lb...............................240g	
	Sugar
1 lb 1.1/2 oz..............................500g	1 oz................................. 2 Tablespoons
	8 oz....................................... 1 cup
16 oz / 1lb................................480g	
	Brown Sugar
2lb 2oz ....1 kilo	3 oz................................. 1/2 cup

Liquid Measures

Imperial	Fl. oz.	Metric	American
2 Tablespoons	1	20 mls.	2 Tblsps.
4 Tablespoons	2	40 mls.	1/4 cup
1/4 pt.	5	150mls	2/3 cup
1/2 pt.	10	300 mls	1.1/4 cups
1 pt	20	600 mls	2. 1/2 cups
1.1/3 pts plus 2 tablespoons		1 litre	4.1/2 cups

(1 U.S. pt = 16 fl. oz = 2 cups)